INTRODUCTION TO ARTIFICIAL INTELLIGENCE AND GENERATIVE AI FOR NOVICE

Exploring Artificial Intelligence Systems and their Applications

Introduction to Artificial Intelligence and Generative AI for Novice Copyright © 2023 by Adam Neural

All rights reserved.

Disclaimer

License Notes

publisher, except in the case of brief quotations embodied in critical reviews and certain other non-commercial uses permitted by copyright law.

Revised Edition Year

Cover Design by Clara

Edited by Clara

Book layout by Clara

Clara, United State

Table of Contents

Introduction

Artificial intelligence (AI) is currently one of the most talked-about and significant modern technologies. It is being utilized more frequently across a wide range of businesses to enhance workflows, offers individualized experiences, and even assist in resolving difficult societal problems. Although AI is becoming more commonplace, many people are still confused about what it is and how it functions. "This book" is useful in this situation.

This manual aims to give a thorough yet understandable introduction to AI. It discusses the development of AI, its various subfields, and its applications in sectors like healthcare, finance, and retail. It also covers the ethical and societal ramifications of AI, such as issues with bias, privacy, and the effect on employment.

The approachability of "This book" is one of its main advantages. The manual's straightforward, concise writing makes it simple for readers to comprehend the ideas without becoming lost in technical jargon. In order to assist readers, apply what they have learned to their own commercial or personal initiatives, it contains real-world examples and useful exercises.

"This book" is the ideal tool for learning more about AI, whether you are a business owner trying to integrate AI into your operations or are just curious about the subject. By the book's conclusion, readers will be well-versed in the foundations of AI and able to use this technology to accomplish their objectives.

It is more crucial than ever to acquire a fundamental understanding of this potent technology in a world where AI is progressively influencing how we conduct our daily lives. With "This book," readers will be well-prepared to traverse the complicated world of artificial intelligence and use it to streamline their lives and accomplish their goals. So, let's get started and together explore the transformational possibilities of AI.

Purpose of The Book and Targeted Audience

The book "Introduction to Artificial Intelligence and Generative Ai For Novice aims to give readers an accessible and digestible introduction to the principles of AI. The book tries to demystify the often scary and overwhelming realm of AI and aid readers in developing a deeper grasp of this quickly developing technology.

The manual is broken up into a number of sections, each of which deals with a different area of AI. It begins with a summary of AI history, including its inception and significant advancements that have influenced the field. After that, it explores the numerous varieties of AI, including supervised learning, unsupervised learning, and reinforcement learning, and offers instances of their practical applications in different fields.

The approachability of "This book" is one of its advantages. Without becoming mired in technical jargon, the book's readers may easily understand the topics because of its simple, succinct writing. The manual provides useful activities that let readers put what they've learned into practice and get first-hand AI experience.

This book is intended at a wide range of readers, regardless of their degree of skill, who are all interested in learning more about artificial intelligence. This book will be especially helpful to business owners and entrepreneurs since it offers real-world examples and exercises for how to apply AI to enhance operations and accomplish goals. The thorough introduction of AI concepts and applications will be helpful to both students and professionals in subjects including data science, engineering, and computer science.

Moreover, this book will be educational and stimulating for everyone who is interested in AI and its possible effects on society. The guide provides readers with a comprehensive grasp of the technology and its implications by examining the ethical and societal ramifications of AI, including worries about prejudice, privacy, and the effect on jobs.

Generally speaking, "This book" is a helpful tool for anyone wishing to get a fundamental grasp of AI and its applications, and is especially helpful for individuals without a technical background. It provides readers with a thorough yet approachable overview to AI, assisting them in navigating this fascinating field's difficult terrain and taking advantage of its transformative potential.

Brief overview of AI and its potential impact on society

Making intelligent computers that are capable of performing activities that traditionally require human intelligence, such as speech recognition, decision-making, and problem-solving, is the focus of artificial intelligence (AI), a fast-developing branch of computer science. Although artificial intelligence has been around for some time, current developments in machine learning, deep learning, and natural language processing have significantly advanced the creation of AI systems.

Healthcare, transportation, manufacturing, and finance are just a few of the sectors that AI has the potential to revolutionize. It can aid companies in decision-making, efficiency enhancement, and the development of new goods and services. AI-powered chatbots, for instance, can assist customers, and machine learning algorithms can analyze data to spot patterns and trends that might guide corporate plans. AI may help doctors diagnose and treat patients, while it can also help with traffic flow and accident reduction in the healthcare and transportation industries.

However, AI also has the potential to have a huge, both beneficial and harmful, impact on society. As computers grow increasingly capable of carrying out tasks that were once performed by humans, one of the key worries surrounding AI is the possible impact on employment. According to some analysts, AI may result in major job displacement, particularly in sectors like manufacturing and transportation. Others counter that AI will lead to new employment prospects and the emergence of new businesses, including those devoted to the creation and upkeep of AI.

The possibility for bias and discrimination in AI systems is a further worry. Biased data can be used to train AI algorithms, which can provide discriminating results. For instance, it has been demonstrated that people with darker skin tones experience higher error rates when using facial recognition technology, which could have detrimental effects on law enforcement and other uses. This raises questions about the possibility that AI will reinforce and magnify current societal biases.

As AI systems proliferate and amass large volumes of data, there are also worries about privacy and security. This data can be analyzed by AI to learn more about specific people, which raises questions about how this data will be utilized and who will have access to it. In the context of social media and other online platforms, where users frequently divulge personal information that may be used for targeted advertising and other purposes, this is especially pertinent.

Overall, even though AI has the potential to significantly benefit society, it is crucial to take into account and solve any potential drawbacks. It is critical to approach the development and deployment of AI with caution and careful thought as it continues to develop and become increasingly interwoven into our lives. This entails making sure AI systems are created with openness and accountability in mind, that any biases are mitigated, and that people's privacy and security are protected.

Overview of the book's structure and key themes.

The book is divided into three main sections, although there are also other major themes that run throughout it. The significance of inter-human cooperation is one of these themes. Although AI has the ability to automate a variety of jobs, it cannot replace the creativity, empathy, and critical thinking that come from being a human. The book places a strong emphasis on the fact that, rather than being used to replace human labor, AI is best used in conjunction with human skill and judgment.

The requirement for openness and responsibility in the creation and application of AI is another important subject. AI systems must be developed and put into use with accountability and transparency in mind as they become more sophisticated and prevalent. This involves making sure AI systems are extensively tested and reviewed before deployment and are subject to continual monitoring and review. Transparency in decision-making procedures is also important.

The significance of ethical considerations in the design and use of AI is also emphasized in the book. This entails tackling problems like bias and discrimination in AI systems, making sure that AI is applied for socially desirable goals, and upholding people's privacy and security. The book examines some of the major ethical issues that arise in the development of AI and offers recommendations for people and organizations that wish to make sure that using AI is morally and responsibly.

In general, the format of "This book: Introduction to Artificial Intelligence and Generative Ai For Novice" is designed to give readers a thorough and understandable review of AI, its applications, and its possible social impacts. The book emphasizes the need for openness, cooperation, and ethical considerations in AI development and deployment and is intended to be a useful resource for anybody who wants to learn about AI and how it may be used for either professional or personal purposes.

PART I:

Understanding AI

CHAPTER ONE

What Is AI?

Artificial intelligence, or AI, is a vast area that includes a variety of methods and strategies for building machines that are capable of carrying out tasks that ordinarily need human intelligence. Fundamentally, AI entails the creation of algorithms and computer programs that can evaluate data, spot patterns, and inform decisions. To increase their accuracy and efficiency over time, these algorithms and programs can be trained using a variety of methods, including machine learning, deep learning, and neural networks.

Making machines that can think, reason, and learn like humans is one of the main aims of AI. This entails creating algorithms and software that can comprehend speech, recognize real language, and even replicate human emotions and behavior. The ultimate goal of AI is to build robots with intelligence equal to or greater than that of humans, and to use these skills to increase productivity, resolve challenging issues, and deepen our understanding of the world.

There are numerous varieties of AI, each with distinct advantages and disadvantages. The most prevalent varieties of AI include:

AI that follows a set of predetermined rules to make decisions and carry out activities is known as rule-based AI. For instance, depending on a set of criteria regarding the kinds of transactions that are likely to be fraudulent, a rule-based AI system could be used to detect fraudulent credit card transactions.

AI that uses machine learning trains algorithms to spot patterns in data and base choices on those patterns. Using supervised learning, unsupervised learning, or reinforcement learning strategies, machine learning algorithms can be trained.

Deep learning is a sort of machine learning that uses neural networks—systems that are modeled after the structure of the human brain—to train algorithms. Deep learning algorithms are able to identify intricate patterns and base choices on them.

Numerous sectors, including healthcare, banking, manufacturing, and transportation, could be completely transformed by AI. AI can be used, for instance, to enhance supply chain management in manufacturing, create more precise and effective medical diagnoses, and optimize financial portfolios and trading techniques.

However, the creation and application of AI also bring up numerous significant societal and ethical concerns. In addition to worries about prejudice and discrimination in AI systems, they include worries about job displacement and the effect of AI on the labor market. These concerns must be properly taken into account as AI develops and becomes more commonplace in our daily lives.

A brief history of AI

Since its inception in the middle of the 20th century, AI has advanced significantly. The creation of intelligent computers that can reason, think, and learn like humans has advanced significantly throughout time. Today, artificial intelligence (AI) is not just a theoretical idea but a fast expanding discipline with practical applications.

Warren McCulloch and Walter Pitts' invention of the first mathematical model of a neural network in 1943 was one of the initial advancements in artificial intelligence. Artificial neural networks, which are now widely utilized in machine learning and deep learning, were made possible as a result of this.

The Turing Test, developed by Alan Turing in 1950, is still used to assess a machine's capacity for intelligent behavior comparable to that of a person. In the test, a human assessor uses a text-based interface to speak with both a machine and a human. The assessor then attempts to identify which is the machine and which is the human.

Many people credit the Dartmouth Conference with establishing artificial intelligence as a formal discipline of research. It took place in 1956. The conference organized a research agenda for the subject and brought together scholars from many fields to talk about the potential of AI.

The first artificial intelligence (AI) program, named the Logic Theorist, was developed by John McCarthy, Marvin Minsky, Nathaniel Rochester, and Claude Shannon in 1958. It was capable of proving mathematical theorems. This demonstrated the capability of machines to carry out challenging reasoning tasks, marking an important milestone in AI research.

The idea of expert systems, which entailed developing computer programs that could render judgments or offer guidance in a particular field of knowledge, was first developed in the 1960s. Expert Systems were employed in a number of industries, including engineering, banking, and medical.

In the 1970s, the focus of AI research switched to knowledge-based systems, which involves applying techniques for knowledge representation and reasoning to build more complex AI systems.

Machine learning methods were introduced to AI research in the 1980s, involving the training of AI systems utilizing big datasets. As a result, techniques like the backpropagation algorithm, which is still frequently employed in deep learning, were created.

The 1990s saw an increase in the use of probabilistic and statistical methods in AI research, which sparked the creation of Bayesian networks and other probabilistic models.

The development of intelligent agents—software programs that can interact with the environment and make decisions based on that interaction—became the emphasis of AI research in the 2000s.

Today, artificial intelligence (AI) is a fast expanding field with applications in a variety of sectors, including manufacturing, healthcare, finance, and transportation. With the emergence of open-source AI frameworks and cloud-based AI services, AI is also becoming more readily available to people and small enterprises. In the coming years, AI is anticipated to have a huge impact on society and have the power to completely transform the way we live and work.

Types of AI

Artificial intelligence (AI) is a fast-developing discipline that includes a variety of methods and strategies. The idea of creating machines that could think like humans was first put forth by computer scientist Alan Turing in the 1940s, which is when AI first began to take shape. Since then, researchers have made important strides in AI, resulting in the creation of numerous distinct types of AI.

A subset of artificial intelligence (AI) called machine learning (ML) uses models and statistical techniques to help systems learn from data. A model is trained on labeled data in supervised learning, when the input and output are both known. For instance, to identify fresh handwritten digits, a machine learning model may be trained on a dataset containing handwritten digits and their related labels. Unsupervised learning involves training a model using data that has not been labeled, thus the input and output are unknown. It is up to the model to determine relationships or patterns in the data on its own. In reinforcement learning, a model is trained by trial and error, with rewards for good judgments and penalties for bad ones.

Deep Learning, a subset of machine learning, uses neural networks to provide systems the ability to learn from data. Multiple layers of interconnected nodes, or neurons, make up neural networks, which are trained on enormous datasets. The network's layers process the data, each layer building on the results of the one before it. As a result, the network can detect data patterns that are getting more complicated. Particularly effective applications of deep learning can be found in computer vision, speech recognition, and natural language processing.

A branch of artificial intelligence called "natural language processing" (NLP) is concerned with how computers and human language interact. NLP uses algorithms and models to give computers the ability to comprehend, decipher, and produce human language. NLP is frequently used in chatbots, sentiment analysis, and machine translation, among other things. With the creation of cutting-edge language models like GPT-3, NLP has improved significantly in recent years.

Robotics is the application of intelligent machines to carry out manual labor. Robotics systems can be as simple as devices that carry out a particular task or as complicated as systems that can learn from experience and adapt to changing situations. From manufacturing to healthcare to space exploration, robotics has various uses.

Expert Systems are artificial intelligence (AI) systems that are intended to replicate the judgment skills of a human expert in a particular field. Expert systems are often rule-based, which means they base their conclusions or recommendations on a set of predetermined rules. For instance, a healthcare expert system might be created to identify illnesses based on the symptoms of a patient.

These are only a few of the various kinds of AI that are now in use. We may anticipate the emergence of new varieties of AI that are more potent and advanced than ever before as AI research continues to advance. Numerous sectors and facets of daily life could be transformed by AI's plethora of possible uses. However, there are also worries about the possible dangers and ethical issues associated with AI, just like there are with any new technology. As AI advances, it is critical to approach the technology with prudence and give careful thought to any potential social effects.

Explanation of how AI works and its potential applications

AI functions by giving computers the ability to learn from data and take actions or complete tasks based on that learning. Data collection, data preparation, model training, and model testing are often included in the process. The ultimate goal of AI is to create systems that are capable of carrying out operations that would typically need human intellect, such as picture recognition, language understanding, prediction making, and decision making.

The ability of AI to process and interpret enormous amounts of data considerably more quickly than a person could is one of its main benefits. This makes it ideal for use in industries where a lot of data is created and needs to be examined fast, like healthcare, finance, and marketing.

A kind of AI called machine learning involves teaching algorithms to spot patterns in data. By learning from the data, they are trained on, these algorithms are made to become more accurate over time. One kind of machine learning is supervised learning, which includes feeding the algorithm with labeled or previously categorized data in order to teach it to spot patterns. On the other hand, unsupervised learning includes training the algorithm on unlabeled data and letting it find patterns on its own.

Neural network training is a component of deep learning, a subclass of machine learning that uses sophisticated algorithms designed to mimic the human brain. Deep learning algorithms can be used for tasks like speech recognition, natural language processing, and image recognition since they are made to find patterns in big datasets of audio or image data.

Another branch of AI that focuses on comprehending and interpreting human language is natural language processing (NLP). In order to extract meaning and context from text and audio data, NLP algorithms examine the data. Applications like chatbots, virtual assistants, and language translation employ this technology.

AI can be applied to the healthcare industry to evaluate medical pictures, help with diagnosis, and create new medicines. In order to find patterns that might be symptomatic of specific diseases or disorders, for instance, machine learning algorithms can be trained on vast databases of medical images. Electronic medical records can be analyzed using AI to find potential drug interactions or negative effects.

AI can be applied to finance to assess market data and decide which investments to make. On the basis of past market data, for instance, machine learning algorithms can be trained to find trends and patterns that might point to profitable investment opportunities. AI can be used to spot risky situations and catch fraudulent transactions.

AI can be used in marketing to analyze client data and create niche advertising campaigns. For instance, to determine the goods or services that customers are most likely to be interested in, machine learning algorithms can be trained on data about customer behavior and preferences. Using AI, social media data can be analyzed to track brand reputation and locate prospective influencers.

These are only a few examples of the potential uses for artificial intelligence. We can anticipate the emergence of fresh, ground-breaking applications across a wide range of industries as technology advances. However, there are also worries about the possible dangers and ethical issues associated with AI, just like there are with any new technology. It is crucial to approach the technology with prudence and take into account any potential negative effects it may have on society, including concerns about issues like job displacement, bias, and privacy.

CHAPTER TWO

How Does AI work?

The field of technology known as artificial intelligence, or AI, is expanding quickly and has the potential to completely change how we live and work. Fundamentally, artificial intelligence (AI) is the process of building intelligent machines that can recognize patterns in data, learn from them, and act accordingly.

Computer scientists originally started investigating the idea of building machines that could perform jobs that would typically need human intelligence in the middle of the 20th century, which is when AI first emerged. Early research in artificial intelligence concentrated on creating rule-based systems, which applied logical rules to solve issues.

Researchers started paying increasing attention to machine learning in the 1980s and 1990s, which includes teaching machines to learn from data using statistical techniques. Through this method, machines were able to interpret natural language, recognize images, and recognize speech.

Deep learning, a potent type of machine learning that includes teaching neural networks—which are designed after the human brain—to learn from a lot of data, has evolved in recent years. This strategy has enabled innovations in fields like speech recognition, computer vision, and natural language processing and has resulted in the creation of AI systems that can perform some tasks better than humans.

From healthcare and banking to transportation and entertainment, AI has the potential to revolutionize a wide range of industries. AI is being used, for instance, in the healthcare industry to provide more precise diagnostic tools, forecast patient outcomes, and enhance medication research.

AI is being applied to banking to identify fraud, examine market trends, and customize client experiences. AI is being applied in the field of transportation to create self-driving vehicles that can decrease accidents and boost productivity.

Despite the potential advantages of AI, there are also worries about its possible hazards and ethical implications. The potential for bias in AI systems, which can result in discrimination and unfair treatment, is a key cause for concern. Concern has also been raised regarding how AI may affect employment as computers become increasingly capable of carrying out formerly performed by humans' duties.

It's critical to approach AI technology cautiously and with regard for its potential social effects as the area of AI develops. This entails addressing concerns like privacy, bias, and job displacement as well as making sure that AI is created and applied in an ethical and responsible way.

Explanation of how AI learns and makes decisions

Deep learning and natural language processing (NLP) are two additional methods that can be employed in the development of AI systems in addition to machine learning.

A part of machine learning called deep learning uses massive datasets to train artificial neural networks. These neural networks can be used for tasks like image and speech recognition, language translation, and playing games like chess or go since they were created to imitate the structure and operation of the human brain. Particularly effective applications of deep learning can be found in computer vision and natural language processing.

The application of artificial intelligence (AI) to the interaction of computers and human languages is known as natural language processing (NLP). NLP entails teaching computer programs to comprehend and produce human language. These programs can then be used for sentiment analysis, chatbots, and language translation, among other things. With several potential applications in industries including customer service, healthcare, and education, NLP is a rapidly expanding field of AI.

Depending on how autonomous they are, AI systems can be divided into many sorts. While some AI systems are created to function with little to no human input, others need human input or supervision. Autonomous vehicles, for instance, are intended to work without the need for human participation, yet virtual personal assistants like Siri or Alexa need on user input to operate.

AI systems are often created to automate human-centric processes like decision-making, language translation, and picture recognition. This might increase productivity, decrease errors, and free up human workers to concentrate on more challenging or innovative jobs. However, there are also worries about how AI will affect employment and its propensity to reinforce prejudice or discrimination.

As AI develops, it is crucial to approach its deployment and development with caution and give careful thought to any potential effects on society. This entails dealing with concerns like data privacy, bias, and responsibility as well as making sure that AI is created and applied in an ethical and responsible way.

An overview of the algorithms and techniques used in AI

AI algorithms and techniques can be broadly categorized into three main types: supervised learning, unsupervised learning, and reinforcement learning.

Supervised learning is a type of machine learning that involves training an AI system using labeled data. The AI system is presented with input data and the corresponding desired output, and the algorithm learns to associate the input with the correct output. For example, an AI system might be trained to recognize handwritten digits by being presented with images of digits along with their corresponding labels.

Unsupervised learning is a type of machine learning that involves training an AI system without labeled data. The system is presented with input data and the algorithm learns to identify patterns or relationships within the data. Unsupervised learning can be used for tasks such as clustering, where the AI system groups similar items together based on their characteristics.

Reinforcement learning is a type of machine learning that involves training an AI system to learn from experience. The system is presented with a task and must learn to maximize a reward signal based on its actions. Reinforcement learning is often used in robotics, where the AI system must learn to navigate a physical environment and interact with objects.

In addition to these broad categories, there are many specific algorithms and techniques used in AI, including:

Neural networks: An artificial neural network is a type of machine learning model that is designed to mimic the structure and function of the human brain. Neural networks can be used for tasks such as image and speech recognition, language translation, and playing games.

Decision trees: A decision tree is a type of algorithm that is used for classification and regression analysis. The algorithm uses a tree-like model of decisions and their possible consequences to create a decision-making process.

Support vector machines: A support vector machine is a type of algorithm that is used for classification and regression analysis. The algorithm works by finding the hyperplane that maximally separates the data points into different classes.

Random forests: A random forest is a type of algorithm that uses multiple decision trees to improve classification and regression accuracy.

Natural language processing: Natural language processing (NLP) is a branch of AI that focuses on the interaction between computers and human languages. NLP involves training algorithms to understand and generate human language, which can be used for tasks such as language translation, chatbots, and sentiment analysis.

Examples of how AI is used in different industries

AI is used in a wide range of industries, from healthcare and finance to manufacturing and transportation. Here are some examples of how AI is used in different industries:

Healthcare: AI is used in healthcare for a variety of purposes, including medical imaging analysis, drug discovery, and personalized medicine. For example, AI-powered medical imaging analysis can help doctors detect diseases such as cancer and Alzheimer's disease at an early stage, which can improve patient outcomes. AI can also be used to predict which treatments will be most effective for individual patients, based on their genetic profile and other factors.

Finance: In finance, AI is used for fraud detection, risk assessment, and investment decision-making. For example, AI-powered fraud detection systems can analyze large amounts of data to identify patterns and anomalies that may indicate fraudulent activity. AI can also be used to analyze financial data to make investment decisions, based on factors such as market trends, company performance, and economic indicators.

Manufacturing: In manufacturing, AI is used for quality control, predictive maintenance, and supply chain optimization. For example, AI-powered quality control systems can analyze images of products to identify defects and ensure that they meet quality standards. AI can also be used to predict when equipment is likely to fail, so that maintenance can be scheduled in advance, which can reduce downtime and save money.

Transportation: In transportation, AI is used for autonomous vehicles, traffic management, and predictive maintenance. For example, self-driving cars use AI to navigate roads and avoid obstacles, while AI-powered traffic management systems can analyze traffic data to optimize routes and reduce congestion. AI can also be used to predict when transportation infrastructure, such as bridges and roads, will need maintenance, so that repairs can be scheduled in advance.

Retail: In retail, AI is used for personalized marketing, inventory management, and customer service. For example, AI-powered recommendation engines can analyze customer data to suggest products that are likely to be of interest to individual shoppers. AI can also be used to optimize inventory levels by predicting demand and identifying the most profitable pricing strategies. In addition, AI-powered chatbots can provide customer service around the clock, answering questions and resolving issues in real-time.

Energy: In the energy sector, AI is used for renewable energy optimization, predictive maintenance, and safety management. For example, AI-powered renewable energy systems can analyze weather patterns and energy demand to optimize the use of solar, wind, and other renewable energy sources. AI can also be used to predict when equipment is likely to fail, so that maintenance can be scheduled in advance, which can reduce downtime and increase safety.

Agriculture: In agriculture, AI is used for crop monitoring, soil analysis, and yield prediction. For example, AI-powered drones and satellites can collect data on crop health and growth patterns, which can be used to optimize irrigation and fertilizer use. AI can also be used to predict crop yields based on factors such as weather patterns and soil composition, which can help farmers make more informed decisions about planting and harvesting.

Education: In education, AI is used for personalized learning, student assessment, and administrative tasks. For example, AI-powered educational software can adapt to the learning style and pace of individual students, providing customized lesson plans and feedback. AI can also be used to analyze student data to identify areas where additional support may be needed. In addition, AI-powered administrative systems can automate tasks such as grading and scheduling, which can free up teachers and administrators to focus on more complex tasks.

These are just a few examples of how AI is being used in various industries. As AI technology continues to evolve, it is likely that we will see even more innovative applications that have the potential to transform the way we work, live, and interact with the world around us.

CHAPTER THREE

Getting Started With AI

AI is a rapidly growing field that encompasses a wide range of tools and technologies. These tools and technologies are used to develop, train, and deploy AI models, as well as to analyze and visualize data. In this section, we will provide an introduction to some of the most commonly used tools and technologies in AI, including programming languages and software frameworks.

Programming Languages: One of the most important tools in AI is programming languages. Some of the most commonly used programming languages in AI include Python, Java, C++, and R. Python is particularly popular because of its ease of use, extensive libraries, and support for popular AI frameworks. Java and C++ are commonly used for developing high-performance AI applications, while R is often used for statistical analysis and data visualization.

Software Frameworks: In addition to programming languages, there are many software frameworks that are used in AI. These frameworks provide pre-built algorithms, tools, and libraries that can be used to develop AI models more quickly and efficiently. Some of the most popular AI frameworks include TensorFlow, PyTorch, and Keras. TensorFlow is an open-source framework developed by Google that is particularly popular for deep learning applications. PyTorch is an open-source machine learning framework that is known for its ease of use and flexibility. Keras is a high-level neural networks API that is designed to be user-friendly and easy to learn.

Data Visualization Tools: Another important tool in AI is data visualization software. Data visualization tools are used to create charts, graphs, and other visualizations that can help analysts and researchers to better understand patterns and trends in data. Some of the most popular data visualization tools include Tableau, Power BI, and ggplot2. Tableau is a powerful data visualization tool that allows users to create interactive dashboards and reports. Power BI is a cloud-based data visualization platform that is particularly popular for business intelligence applications. ggplot2 is an open-source data visualization library for the R programming language that allows users to create publication-quality visualizations.

These are just a few of the many tools and technologies that are used in AI. As AI continues to grow and evolve, it is likely that we will see new and innovative tools and technologies emerge that will further advance the field.

How to get started with building your own AI system.

Although creating your own AI system can be challenging, anyone can get started with the appropriate strategy. To start creating your own AI system, follow these steps:

Establish your project's objectives: The first stage is to decide what issue your AI system will be used to address. Anything from predicting stock prices to identifying spam emails could fall under this category. You can start considering the kind of data you need and the necessary methods after you are clear on the purpose of your project.

Collect and clean your data: Since data is the backbone of all artificial intelligence systems, this is the next stage. You could need to get information from a variety of sources, including databases, APIs, and web scraping, depending on the objectives of your project. As this will help assure the correctness of your AI model, it is crucial to make sure the data is clean and consistent.

Choose an AI framework from the many options available; each has advantages and disadvantages. TensorFlow, PyTorch, and Keras are a few of the most well-liked AI frameworks. You must pick a framework that is suitable for your project and with which you are at ease working.

Once you have the data and the architecture for your AI system, you can begin training your AI model. Using your data, you may train your model to spot trends and anticipate outcomes. To identify the ideal set of parameters and methods for your project, you will need to experiment.

Test and improve your model: After your AI model has been trained, you must put it to the test to make sure it is precise and trustworthy. Your model might need to be modified and retrained in order to produce the intended outcomes.

The last stage is to deploy your AI system so that it can be used in practical situations. This can entail incorporating your model into an already-in-use software program or creating a brand-new program specifically for your model.

Select the appropriate hardware: Since AI models need a lot of computing power, it's critical to select the appropriate hardware for your model. This can entail utilizing a powerful GPU or purchasing a cloud-based platform with scalable compute resources.

Recognize the AI system's limitations: AI systems have limits and are not flawless. It's crucial to be aware of these restrictions and to use your system only in circumstances where it can be trusted. An AI system that forecasts stock prices, for instance, could not be appropriate for making investment decisions since it is unable to take into consideration all the variables that affect stock prices.

Follow the most recent AI developments: AI is a topic that is always developing thanks to the constant creation of new approaches and algorithms. It's critical to stay current with advancements and, where appropriate, incorporate them into your AI system.

The ethical and legal ramifications of your system should be taken into account because AI systems have the ability to have a significant impact on society. For instance, you must ensure that your AI system is impartial and discriminatory if it is used for hiring or recruitment.

Although creating your own AI system can be exciting, it's necessary to proceed with care and an open mind. You can create a strong and efficient AI system that can actually change the world by following these procedures and keeping these things in mind.

PART II

Applying AI

CHAPTER FOUR

Using AI in Business

Business operations have been changed by AI, which offers strong tools and strategies for resolving complicated issues and accomplishing strategic objectives. One of AI's main benefits is its capacity to swiftly and accurately evaluate enormous amounts of data, producing insights that would be challenging or impossible for humans to find.

One of the most often used uses of AI in the corporate world is in customer support. Artificial intelligence (AI)-powered chatbots and virtual assistants can offer clients quick, efficient support by responding to their inquiries and guiding them to the data they require. By lessening the workload on human support employees, this can increase customer satisfaction and free them up to work on more challenging problems.

AI is also being used by corporations for predictive analytics. AI systems can make precise predictions about the future by looking at historical data to find patterns and trends. This can be especially helpful in fields like finance, where precise predictions can help with risk management and smarter investment choices.

AI can also be applied to boost organizational effectiveness. AI, for instance, can assist in optimizing delivery routes in logistics, cutting down on the time and expense needed to convey items. Artificial intelligence (AI) in manufacturing can assist in identifying production process inefficiencies and suggesting modifications that might help decrease waste and boost output.

Another industry where AI is having a significant impact is marketing. AI systems can assist firms in delivering targeted and customized advertising messages that are more likely to connect with certain customers by evaluating customer data. This can aid companies in increasing conversion rates and maximizing the return on their advertising investments.

Of course, adopting AI in business comes with its share of difficulties. The quality of the data is one of the main obstacles. In order for AI systems to produce correct insights, they need a lot of high-quality data, yet many businesses find it difficult to successfully gather and manage this data. There are also worries about data security and privacy, as well as the possibility that AI will replace human workers.

The advantages of applying AI to business are obvious, despite these difficulties. Businesses who are able to use AI to enhance their operations, customer experiences, and marketing initiatives are likely to have a considerable competitive edge over those that are unable to do so. Businesses will need to keep on top of the most recent advancements in technology as well as devise fresh, creative methods to use AI for growth and success.

An overview of how AI is being used in different business functions, including marketing, sales, and operations

A wide range of industries, including healthcare, finance, and retail, are being transformed by AI. Businesses are looking at new ways to leverage AI as it continues to advance to increase productivity, efficiency, and innovation across all facets of their operations.

Marketing: The capacity to give personalized content and recommendations to clients is one of the most important effects of AI on marketing. Artificial intelligence (AI) algorithms can produce insights that can help organizations enhance their marketing efforts by evaluating enormous volumes of customer data and activity. In order to spot trends and send customized marketing messages to particular people or groups, this includes evaluating data from social media, web surfing activity, and purchase history.

AI is being used in marketing to automate repetitive processes, such as email marketing campaigns, social media posting, and ad targeting, in addition to personalized marketing. This can increase the efficiency of a company's marketing activities while saving time and money.

Sales: By automating repetitive operations, enhancing lead creation, and offering predictive insights, AI is also being utilized to improve sales performance. Sales teams may prioritize leads, create precise projections, and find chances for cross-selling and upselling with the use of AI-powered sales tools.

Chatbots powered by AI can help sales organizations by responding quickly to client inquiries and addressing routine customer inquiries, freeing up sales personnel to concentrate on more difficult work.

Operations: To increase productivity, cut expenses, and streamline procedures, AI is being applied in operations. Robots and machines with AI capabilities can automate repetitive operations in the manufacturing industry, improving productivity and quality while lowering human costs. AI algorithms in logistics can streamline the shipping process, cutting costs and shipment times while increasing customer satisfaction.

AI is being employed in customer care to offer customers speedy and effective assistance. Routine questions can be instantly answered by AI-powered chatbots, while more difficult questions can be escalated to human agents. This can speed up response times and lower customer support expenses.

Finance: Routine financial processes like fraud detection and risk management are being automated using artificial intelligence (AI). AI algorithms are capable of analyzing large volumes of data from many sources, such as consumer behavior and financial transactions, to spot patterns and anomalies that might be signs of fraud. This can increase the precision of firms' fraud detection efforts while saving time and money.

AI is now being utilized in finance to give customers individualized financial advice. In order to create customized investment strategies that can assist clients reach their financial objectives, AI algorithms can examine customer data, including risk tolerance and investment goals.

Healthcare: By increasing the precision of medical diagnoses, lowering healthcare expenses, and enhancing patient outcomes, AI is also revolutionizing the healthcare sector. In order to find trends and provide precise diagnoses, AI systems can scan enormous amounts of patient data, including medical pictures and electronic health records.

AI is also employed in the medical field to create individualized treatment regimens for patients. Based on each patient's medical history, genetic composition, and other characteristics, AI systems can assess patient data to recommend the most suitable treatments.

Practical guidance on how to use **AI** to improve business processes and decision-making

Artificial intelligence (AI) has become a powerful tool in the business world, helping companies improve their operations, customer experience, and decision-making. However, it can be challenging for businesses to know where to start and how to integrate AI into their existing processes.

Here are some practical tips on how to use AI to improve your business processes and decision-making:

Identify the areas where AI can have the most impact: Start by assessing your business processes and identifying the areas where AI can have the most significant impact. For example, you might want to use AI to optimize your supply chain, improve your customer service, or analyze your data to gain insights into customer behavior.

1. **Choose the right AI solution:** Once you have identified the areas where AI can have the most impact, you need to choose the right AI solution for your business. There are many different types of AI solutions available, such as chatbots, predictive analytics, and natural language processing. Choose the one that best suits your business needs.

2. **Get the right data:** AI relies on large amounts of data to learn and make predictions. Therefore, you need to ensure that you have access to high-quality data that is relevant to your business processes. This might require you to invest in data collection and storage infrastructure.

3. **Work with experts:** Implementing AI can be complex, and it's essential to work with experts who have experience in the field. You may want to consider

hiring a data scientist or partnering with an AI consultancy to help you implement AI effectively.

4. **Test and iterate:** AI is not a one-time implementation. It's essential to test and iterate your AI solution to ensure that it's working effectively and improving your business processes. Monitor your AI solution's performance regularly and make adjustments as necessary.

5. **Consider the ethical implications:** AI raises ethical concerns, such as bias and privacy. Ensure that you consider these implications when implementing AI in your business processes. Work with your AI experts to ensure that your AI solution is fair, transparent, and complies with relevant regulations.

AI has the power to completely change how businesses function and make decisions. Businesses must have a clear grasp of how to use AI in their particular business context, though, in order to fully fulfill this promise. Businesses can utilize artificial intelligence (AI) to enhance operations, make better decisions, and gain a competitive advantage in their market by adhering to best practices and utilizing the appropriate tools and technology.

CHAPTER FIVE

Using AI in Everyday Life

Artificial intelligence (AI) is getting more and more ingrained in our daily lives as it develops. AI is already everywhere, from virtual personal assistants like Siri and Alexa to recommendation systems used by streaming services and e-commerce sites. This section will examine the practical applications of AI and their potential social repercussions.

Virtual personal assistants are one of the most prevalent ways AI is employed in daily life. Natural language processing (NLP) is a technique used by these AI-powered assistants, like Siri, Alexa, and Google Assistant, to comprehend and reply to user requests. They can assist us with activities like scheduling appointments, setting reminders, and providing information. With the advent of machine learning algorithms that enable them to learn and adapt to user behavior over time, virtual personal assistants are getting more intelligent.

Algorithms for making recommendations are another area where AI is being applied. Based on a user's prior behavior, these algorithms employ data analysis and machine learning to make recommendations for content or products. On streaming services like Netflix and music websites like Spotify, we can observe this in action. These algorithms can provide individualized recommendations based on a user's viewing or listening history, which can increase user engagement and happiness.

AI is being applied in the retail sector to enhance the customer experience. AI-powered chatbots can manage client enquiries and complaints, offering prompt and effective service. Customers may receive product recommendations based on their browsing and purchasing history thanks to AI-powered product recommendations, which are similar to those seen in streaming services. Retailers may benefit from an uptick in sales and improved clientele.

AI is additionally being applied in medicine to enhance patient outcomes. In order to find patterns and trends, machine learning algorithms can examine patient data and medical records. These findings can help with disease diagnosis and therapy. Remote monitoring systems, which use AI to monitor patients, can assist healthcare professionals in keeping tabs on patients and identifying potential problems before they arise.

Concerns regarding AI's effects on society are there, as they are with any new technology. Because AI is being utilized more and more to automate processes that were once done by people, job displacement is one issue to be concerned about. However, AI proponents contend that it can generate new employment prospects in industries that are involved in the development and application of AI.

The potential for AI systems to reinforce prejudice and bigotry is another issue. AI algorithms may make decisions that maintain current societal disparities if they were trained on biased data. This emphasizes how crucial it is to guarantee that AI systems be developed and put into use in an ethical and open manner.

With applications in personal assistants, recommendation systems, retail, healthcare, and more, AI is becoming more and more ingrained in our daily lives. Although there are worries about how AI will affect society, it cannot be denied that technology has the potential to increase productivity, accuracy, and personalization. It will be crucial to make sure that AI is implemented in an ethical and transparent way as it continues to develop.

How AI Is Being Used In Everyday Life, Including Virtual Assistants, Smart Homes, And Self-Driving Cars

Our daily lives are being influenced by artificial intelligence (AI), from our smartphones to our homes, cars, and even businesses. Virtual assistants like Siri, Alexa, and Google Assistant are among the most well-known applications of AI in modern life. These virtual assistants first understand and interpret our requests using natural language processing (NLP), after which they utilize machine learning algorithms to give us pertinent information or perform actions like setting reminders, placing calls, or managing smart home devices.

Speaking of smart homes, AI technology is enhancing their automation and productivity. Artificial intelligence (AI) algorithms are used by smart home appliances like thermostats, lightbulbs, and security systems to learn our routines and preferences and then make appropriate adjustments. To save energy, a smart thermostat, for instance, may figure out when we usually leave the house and alter the temperature accordingly. Similar to that, a smart security system can spot suspicious activities and notify us via our cellphones.

Another example of how AI is applied in daily life is self-driving cars. These vehicles navigate the roadways, recognize obstructions and pedestrians, and make judgments in real-time using a combination of sensors, cameras, and AI algorithms. Although they are not yet extensively used, self-driving cars are now being tested around the globe, and experts believe that they will soon be more prevalent.

AI is also being applied to medical research to create more individualized patient treatments. AI algorithms may find patterns and correlations by examining vast volumes of patient data, which enables doctors to make more precise diagnoses and prescribe more efficient therapies. AI systems, for instance, can examine medical photos to find early indications of cancer or forecast the likelihood of a heart attack.

AI is being employed in the entertainment sector to give consumers more immersive experiences. For instance, AI algorithms are used by streaming services like Netflix and Amazon Prime to suggest movies and TV episodes based on our viewing interests and history. Similar to this, AI is used by video game makers to build NPCs that are more intelligent and resemblant of real people and can converse with players in a more natural manner.

In general, AI is affecting our daily lives more and more, and this trend will continue in the years to come. Although there are worries about the ethical and societal effects of AI, there is no doubting that it has the ability to improve the quality, safety, and ease of our lives.

Practical Guidance on How To Use AI To Improve Everyday Life

Since its inception, AI has advanced significantly and is now a crucial aspect of our daily life. AI is enhancing our lives in a variety of ways, including in our homes, cars, and smartphones. This section will examine how artificial intelligence is utilized in daily life and offer helpful advice on how to use AI to make our daily activities better.

Virtual helpers:

Virtual assistants are one of the most well-liked and frequently utilized uses of AI in modern life. Most people now have one on their smartphone or smart home gadget because they are so commonplace. These assistants, like Siri, Alexa, and Google Assistant, use machine learning and natural language processing to comprehend and carry out spoken orders. In addition to playing music and setting reminders, they can also order groceries and operate smart household appliances. Learn how to use virtual assistants efficiently to get the most out of them by creating customized routines, establishing connections with other smart home devices, and utilizing their special capabilities.

Modern homes:

A simple voice command or a few taps on a smartphone are all it takes for homeowners to operate their appliances, lighting, heating, and security systems in AI-powered smart homes. Our lives are made more comfortable and energy-efficient by smart home devices, which employ sensors and machine learning algorithms to learn about human preferences. With the help of smart home technology, homeowners may automate tedious jobs, reduce their energy costs, and improve their quality of life in general. To get the most out of a smart home setup, it's critical to comprehend the many kinds of smart home gadgets and how they work together.

Autonomous Vehicles:

Self-driving automobiles are arguably the most sophisticated use of AI in modern society. They assess their surroundings and make quick judgments like accelerating, braking, and turning using a variety of sensors, like as radar, lidar, and cameras. It is possible that self-driving cars will change how we commute, making it safer, more effective, and less stressful. However, because this technology is still in its early stages, it's critical to be aware of its constraints and potential dangers, such as cyberattacks, mishaps, and legal complications.

Healthcare:

AI is also employed in healthcare to lower expenses and enhance patient outcomes. In order to aid clinicians in making more precise diagnoses and creating individualized treatment regimens, machine learning algorithms can examine patient data such as medical histories and test results. Patients may monitor their diseases, ask questions, and make appointments with the aid of AI-powered chatbots and virtual nurses. To preserve patient privacy and safety, it is crucial to make sure that these technologies are secure, dependable, and compliant with legal requirements.

Education:

AI is also being applied in education to individualize instruction and enhance student performance. Software designed for adaptive learning can evaluate student performance and offer personalized comments and suggestions. Chatbots powered by AI can also assist students with their schoolwork and provide information. To make sure that pupils get a well-rounded education, it's crucial to combine technology and interpersonal engagement.

Our daily lives have already been significantly improved by AI, and there is still a tremendous amount of room for growth and innovation. It's critical to maintain awareness of potential risks and limitations, learn how to use the technology effectively, and stay informed in order to get the most out of AI in daily life. By doing this, we may fully realize AI's promise and improve our daily lives.

CHAPTER SIX

Ethical Considerations in AI

The ethical ramifications of using AI are a subject of growing concern as it develops and becomes more pervasive. Although AI has immense potential, it can also be utilized in ways that are harmful to people or society at large. As a result, it is crucial to take ethics into account when developing and deploying AI. Bias is one of the biggest ethical issues with AI. The quality of AI systems depends on the data they are trained on. The AI system will be biased if the data is prejudiced. This may lead to people being treated unfairly because of their color, gender, or other traits. For instance, a facial recognition system that was trained primarily using data from white people could have trouble correctly identifying people of color.

The prospect for employment displacement in AI is another ethical issue. There is a chance that many jobs could be automated as AI advances, which would lead to job losses. This might have a big impact on the economy, especially for people who depend on lower-skilled occupations that are most susceptible to automation.

Another important ethical issue with AI is privacy. Large volumes of personal data are frequently needed by AI systems in order for them to work properly. This information has the risk of being misused or exploited, either by the companies creating and implementing the AI systems or by bad actors who are successful in breaking into these systems.

Accountability and transparency are also crucial ethical factors in AI. It can be challenging to comprehend how AI systems decide as they become more complicated. If the AI system delivers biased or damaging results, it may be difficult to hold organizations accountable because to the lack of transparency.

The issue of autonomous AI systems is another one. These systems have the ability to make judgments without the involvement of a person, raising concerns that they can be applied in harmful or unethical ways. An autonomous weapon, for instance, may be deployed to target people without supervision or human involvement.

It is crucial that AI development and deployment be done with care and deliberation in light of these ethical constraints. Organizations creating and implementing AI systems must take precautions to guarantee that these systems are open, impartial, and do not negatively impact people or society as a whole. The creation of regulatory frameworks by politicians is also necessary to guarantee the moral and responsible usage of AI.

ETHICAL CONSIDERATIONS SURROUNDING AI, INCLUDING THE POTENTIAL FOR BIAS AND THE IMPACT ON PRIVACY

Artificial intelligence (AI) has the power to drastically change industries, increase productivity, and vastly enhance people's lives. However, it also creates ethical questions, much like any strong technology. It is vital to address these ethical issues and make sure that the technology is created and used in a responsible and ethical manner as AI gets more and more interwoven into our daily lives.

The potential for prejudice is one of the primary ethical issues with AI. The data that AI systems are taught on determines how objective they are. An artificial intelligence system will be biased if the data it was trained on is skewed. Certain groups of people may experience discriminatory outcomes as a result, which would only serve to reinforce social injustices already in place. For instance, a hiring procedure that favors male candidates may be perpetuated by an AI-powered recruiting system that was educated on prior hiring data.

The effect of AI on privacy is a further matter of ethical concern. Massive volumes of data about people are gathered and processed by AI systems, frequently without that people's awareness or consent. These records may contain private information like names and addresses as well as delicate information like medical histories and biometric information. If this information ends up in the wrong hands, it might be exploited maliciously for things like targeted advertising or identity theft.

AI's effects on jobs and the economy are also a source of worry, in addition to issues with bias and privacy. In some industries, when AI systems improve in capability and replace human labor, job displacement and economic inequality may result. Additionally, AI has the potential to be exploited for evil, such as in autonomous weaponry or deepfake films that may be propagandized.

It is crucial for AI developers and users to approach the technology responsibly and ethically in order to meet these ethical concerns. This entails safeguarding individual privacy, ensuring that AI systems are educated on unbiased data, and taking into account any potential effects on jobs and the economy. Additionally, it calls for accountability and openness in the creation and application of AI systems, as well as detailed explanations of how the systems function and how decisions are made.

In order to ensure the ethical development and application of AI, governments and regulatory organizations must also play a part. This can involve establishing rules and legislation to safeguard people's privacy and stop discrimination, as well as guidelines for the design and application of AI systems.

Despite the enormous potential for AI to improve our lives, it is crucial to discuss the ethical issues that surround the technology. We can make sure that the technology is used to benefit society as a whole, without maintaining existing disparities or abusing individual rights and privacy, by adopting a responsible and ethical approach to the development and use of AI systems.

How to Ensure That AI Is Used in A Responsible and Ethical Way

For individuals, businesses, and governments alike, it's crucial to ensure that AI is used responsibly and ethically. Here are several doable strategies to guarantee the moral application of AI:

Recognize that bias exists and that it has the ability to treat people or groups unfairly. It's critical to recognize and take action to reduce the potential causes of bias in AI systems, such as biased data sets and algorithmic conclusions. This can entail frequently checking AI systems for prejudice and making sure that diverse teams are involved in their development and testing.

Protect your privacy: AI systems have the potential to collect and use enormous amounts of personal data, which raises privacy concerns. Strong data privacy regulations, including data encryption, data minimization, and informed consent for data collection and usage, must be put in place to ensure the ethical use of AI.

Ensure transparency: AI systems are frequently opaque, which makes it challenging to comprehend how they decide. It's crucial to make sure AI systems are open to explanation in order to assure its ethical use. This may entail laying out in detail how the AI system operates and how it came to a particular conclusion.

Think about the effect on society: AI use may have a big effects on society, including the possibility of job loss, economic inequality, and other social repercussions. It's crucial to take into account the potential effects on society and take precautions to lessen any bad effects to ensure the ethical use of AI.

Create an ethical framework: Governments and organizations can create an ethical framework and rules for the creation and application of AI. These frameworks can offer direction on topics like bias, privacy, transparency, and the influence of AI on society.

Engage stakeholders: A variety of stakeholders, including AI experts, policymakers, civil society organizations, and impacted persons or communities, must be consulted in order to ensure the ethical use of AI. AI can be utilized responsibly and ethically by involving these stakeholders in its development and application.

Last but not least, it's critical to consistently assess and upgrade AI systems to make sure they continue to adhere to moral standards. This can entail doing routine audits, taking into account stakeholder comments, and modifying the AI system as necessary to meet any emerging ethical issues.

Part III:

The Future of AI

CHAPTER SEVEN

The Future of AI

The future of AI is a broad and complicated subject that includes many different technology, applications, and ethical issues. I'll go into more detail on some of the major advancements and trends that are influencing the direction of AI in this response.

Higher Adoption

The rising adoption of AI technology across numerous industries is one of the most important trends in the field of artificial intelligence. AI used to be primarily the purview of established tech giants and academic organizations. But in recent years, smaller businesses and even lone coders have had easier access to AI. A wide variety of AI-powered goods and services have sprung up as a result of the democratization of AI, from chatbots and virtual assistants to fraud detection systems and recommendation engines.

As more businesses begin to see the advantages of AI and make investments in AI technologies, this trend is anticipated to continue in the years to come. According to a Gartner estimate, global spending on AI is anticipated to increase from $58 billion in 2020 to $300 billion by 2024.

Natural language processing (NLP) advances

A crucial aspect of artificial intelligence (AI) called natural language processing (NLP) aims to make it possible for machines to comprehend and interpret human language. Thanks to improvements in deep learning algorithms and the availability of enormous volumes of text data, NLP has advanced significantly in recent years.

The introduction of pre-trained language models, like Open AI's GPT series and Google's BERT, is one of the most interesting advances in NLP. These models have shown outstanding results on a variety of NLP tasks, including sentiment analysis, language translation, and text summarization.

It is anticipated that as these models advance, more advanced conversational agents, chatbots, and virtual assistants will be made possible. By understanding and interpreting complicated language, for instance, future chatbots may be able to participate in more natural and contextually appropriate interactions with people.

Ethics-Related Matters

Concern over the ethical ramifications of AI use is growing as technology becomes more commonplace in society. To guarantee that AI is utilized in a responsible and accountable manner, many organizations are attempting to build ethical frameworks for AI development and implementation.

Bias in AI systems is one of the most urgent ethical issues. The data that AI systems are educated on determines how impartial they are, therefore if the data is biased, the system will also be biased. This may result in negative consequences like racial or gender prejudice.

Many organizations are striving to create algorithms that are more resistant to prejudice as well as datasets that are more diverse and representative in order to address this problem. A developing effort also aims to make AI systems accessible and explicable so that users may comprehend how the system came to its conclusions.

Independent Systems

Autonomous systems driven by AI, like self-driving cars and drones, are proliferating. Numerous other industries, including logistics and transportation, could be completely transformed by these systems.

In particular, self-driving automobiles are anticipated to have a big impact on society in the years to come. They may lessen road congestion, promote safety, and give those who are unable to drive—such as the elderly and disabled—more mobility.

Before self-driving cars are used extensively, there are, nevertheless, a number of fundamental obstacles to be addressed. These include technical difficulties like creating reliable object detection and avoidance algorithms as well as regulatory and legal difficulties like figuring out who is responsible for an accident.

Applications in Healthcare

By enabling more precise diagnoses, individualized treatment regimens, and improved patient outcomes, AI has the potential to revolutionize healthcare. There have been a lot of intriguing advancements in this field, including the application of AI in patient monitoring, medical imaging, and drug discovery.

AI-powered medical imaging tools, for instance, are already used to identify and treat diseases like cancer and Alzheimer's.

An Exploration of Future AI

Modernization of Machine Learning

Machine learning, a branch of artificial intelligence, teaches computers to learn from data without explicit programming, as was already indicated. The accuracy of machine learning models has considerably increased as a result of recent developments in deep learning algorithms and the accessibility of massive datasets. Future advancements in machine learning will make it possible for AI to solve more challenging issues and generate forecasts that are more accurate.

Reinforcement learning is one field of machine learning that is expanding quickly. AI models are trained by trial and error using reinforcement learning, which entails giving feedback on the model's activities. In fields like robotics, where AI models may learn to carry out difficult tasks like grabbing and manipulating items, this strategy has shown potential.

Growing Use of AI in Industries

Healthcare, banking, and manufacturing are just a few of the sectors where artificial intelligence is already in use. As businesses try to take use of AI's advantages to boost production, efficiency, and customer experience, we may anticipate seeing an increase in the adoption of AI across a variety of industries in the future.

AI is being utilized in the healthcare sector to examine medical images and support diagnosis. Virtual assistants with AI capabilities are also being deployed to give patients individualized care and support. Artificial intelligence (AI) is utilized in the financial sector for trading, risk management, and fraud detection. AI is being utilized in manufacturing for supply chain efficiency, quality control, and predictive maintenance.

AI Development in New Fields

AI is not only used in the digital sphere. Future applications of AI in new industries like agriculture, transportation, and energy are something we can anticipate.

Drones with AI capabilities can be used in agriculture to monitor crop health and improve irrigation. AI algorithms can also be used to optimize planting and harvesting schedules and predict weather trends. Autonomous cars are being developed for transportation that employ AI to navigate and avoid hazards. AI is being utilized in the energy sector to estimate maintenance needs for power plants and renewable energy sources.

Ethical Issues

Concerns over AI's ethical ramifications are developing as technology becomes more commonplace. For instance, there are worries about the influence of AI on privacy and the possibility that it could replace jobs.

It's true that some jobs might be mechanized by AI, which would result in employment displacement. The development and upkeep of AI, for example, are likely to generate new employment opportunities. It will be crucial to make sure that AI models are trained on a variety of datasets and that the decision-making process is transparent in order to allay worries about bias in AI systems. It will be crucial to develop rules and guidelines for the collecting, storage, and use of personal data by AI systems in order to protect people's privacy.

Cooperation between AI and humans

Although there are worries that AI will replace occupations, in reality, human capabilities will probably be enhanced rather than replaced by AI. We can anticipate increased human-AI collaboration in the future, when AI helps people make decisions and solve problems.

For instance, in the healthcare industry, AI can help doctors diagnose diseases by examining patient data and medical imaging. By examining market patterns and consumer information, artificial intelligence (AI) in finance can help financial advisors make investment suggestions. AI in manufacturing can help engineers by evaluating data from sensors and other sources to optimize production operations.

Natural language processing innovations

Another area of artificial intelligence (AI) called natural language processing (NLP) focuses on teaching computers to comprehend and produce human language. AI models can now do tasks like language translation, sentiment analysis, and chatbot interaction thanks to recent developments in NLP.

We can anticipate more NLP improvements in the future.

Ethical Implications of These Emerging Trends and Predictions.

Artificial intelligence and automation: These technologies are being employed more frequently in sectors like manufacturing, transportation, and healthcare. Although these technologies have the potential to boost production and efficiency, they also raise moral questions concerning worker displacement and the possibility of algorithmic bias. Concerns exist regarding the potential for these technologies to be abused, such as through the deployment of autonomous weapons in conflict. It is crucial to make sure AI and automation are created and deployed in ways that promote human well-being, including ensuring that everyone has fair and equitable access to work opportunities and preventing bias in algorithms.

Big data and privacy: The gathering and analysis of vast amounts of data has turned into a major force in the advancement of new technologies in industries like healthcare, banking, and advertising. Big data usage, however, brings up moral questions regarding data use, consent, and privacy. It is important to make sure that people have control over their personal data and are aware of how it is used. Additionally, it's important to make sure that algorithms and decision-making processes are open and responsible and do not support discrimination or other types of bias.

Genetic engineering and biotechnology: These developments have the potential to revolutionize both agriculture and healthcare. The potential for unintended repercussions, the effect on the environment, and the possibility of genetically-based discrimination are all ethical issues that these technologies also bring up. The development and application of these technologies must prioritize individual health and wellbeing while also taking into account broader societal and environmental concerns.

Sustainability and climate change: Both of these problems are global in scope and call for coordinated action. These difficulties also bring up moral concerns regarding environmental stewardship, justice, and fairness. There is a need to make sure that future generations or vulnerable groups do not bear an unfair share of the burden of combating climate change and promoting sustainability. Additionally, it's important to make sure that people and organizations accept responsibility for their environmental impact and act to lessen it.

Both augmented reality and virtual reality

Technologies for virtual and augmented reality are being used more frequently in industries like entertainment, education, and healthcare. The possibility for addiction, the blending of reality and fantasy, and the effects on mental health are ethical issues raised by these technologies. It is crucial to make sure that these technologies are created and applied in a way that prioritizes human welfare and does not encourage negative attitudes or habits.

Overall, the ethical ramifications of new predictions and trends are intricate and varied. It is crucial to make sure that these technologies are created and used in ways that emphasize human well-being, advance social justice, and are long-term sustainable as they continue to develop and impact our society. To ensure that ethical considerations are at the forefront of the creation and adoption of new technologies, this calls for continual communication and collaboration between technology developers, legislators, and the general public.

How to Shape the Future of AI in A Positive Way?

Ethics rules: As AI become increasingly widespread in our lives, it's critical to have ethical rules in place to guarantee that AI development and use are ethical and advantageous for society. Stakeholders from various backgrounds, such as business executives, academics, government officials, and civil society organizations, may participate in the formulation of ethical standards. These rules should address issues with bias, data protection, privacy, accountability, and openness. In order to prevent the unethical and dangerous use of AI technology, governments and international organizations can also play a significant role in establishing the rules and regulations that govern AI development and application.

Education and awareness: Encouraging public understanding and opinion of AI can be done by promoting education and awareness about the technology. Education for both technical and non-technical audiences, including those for students, teachers, policymakers, and the general public, might fall under this category. Education about the potential advantages and dangers of AI can support its responsible development and application. Promoting AI education and training can also assist alleviate the scarcity of qualified AI workers and give people the know-how and abilities required to work with AI technologies.

Collaboration and partnerships: Collaboration between enterprises, governments, and civil society organizations can support the creation and application of AI that is used responsibly. Governments may support the development of safe, moral, and societally useful AI technology by collaborating with business and academics. Partnerships can encourage cooperation and knowledge-sharing between various industries, which can assist spur innovation and advancement in the field of AI.

Human-centered design: The development and use of AI should be based on the needs and values of people. This can help guarantee that AI is developed and applied in ways that are advantageous to society as a whole. Diverse voices from various racial, ethnic, and socioeconomic backgrounds can be included in the development process as part of a human-centered approach to AI. This strategy may also include creating AI systems that are transparent, understandable, and accountable in order to increase public confidence in them.

Diversity and inclusion: Fostering diversity and inclusion can help minimize bias and guarantee that AI is created in a fair and equitable manner. Promoting diversity in the AI workforce and making sure the data used to train AI systems is varied and representative can both contribute to this. Furthermore, it's crucial to guarantee that AI systems are auditable and bias-tested in order to rectify any potential problems.

Continuous observation and assessment: In order to make sure that AI systems are operating safely and as intended, they need be regularly observed and assessed. This may entail keeping an eye out for prejudice, privacy concerns, and unforeseen effects.

Any faults with AI systems can be quickly identified and fixed with the help of continuous evaluation. Furthermore, openness in the development and application of AI helps foster confidence in these systems and guarantee that they are being put to good use.

In conclusion, cooperation between individuals, groups, and governments is necessary to positively influence the development of AI. We can make sure that AI is created and used in ways that benefit society as a whole by creating ethical guidelines and regulations, promoting education and awareness, encouraging collaboration and partnerships, adopting a human-centered approach, promoting diversity and inclusion, and continuously monitoring and evaluating AI systems.

CHAPTER EIGHT

Legal Implication of AI

In several legal fields, artificial intelligence (AI) has major legal repercussions. It is critical to comprehend the potential legal issues that can emerge as AI technologies develop and become more ingrained in our daily lives.

The following are some of the most significant legal effects of AI:

Intellectual property: Because AI technology has the potential to generate new products or works of art, it raises complicated legal issues regarding who is entitled to the creations' intellectual property rights. Who, for instance, is the legal owner of a picture produced by an AI algorithm? The question of who owns the patent rights for a product created by an AI system is similar. These issues are still up for discussion and call for a greater comprehension of both the law and AI technology.

Privacy: In order for AI systems to work properly, they frequently need access to vast amounts of data, which raises concerns about how to safeguard people's right to privacy. Personal information that can be used to identify and monitor people, such as location data, browser history, and biometric data, can be gathered, stored, and analyzed by AI algorithms. Sensitive personal information may potentially be revealed as a result of data breaches, with serious repercussions for individuals. In order to safeguard people's personal information from abuse and unlawful access, privacy laws must be updated and enforced.

Determining responsibility for an AI system's harm or damages can be challenging because it may fall on the designers, programmers, and users of the system as well. Who is accountable for the damages, for instance, if an accident is caused by an autonomous vehicle? Which comes first, the creator or the user? Determining culpability and responsibility in this matter still needs serious thought and legal knowledge.

Work: AI may result in job displacement and the emergence of new work categories. This can raise concerns about how to defend workers' rights and guarantee that they are fairly compensated. For instance, the rise of automation may make some jobs obsolete and cause unemployment. On the other hand, new occupations like data analysts, AI trainers, and algorithm designers might emerge. Therefore, it is crucial to take into account the legal effects of AI on employment and make sure that workers' rights are safeguarded.

Discrimination: AI systems have the potential to reinforce and magnify biases in a variety of contexts, including hiring, credit scoring, and sentencing for crimes, among others. Individuals and communities may suffer unfair treatment as a result, as well as harm. An AI algorithm that was educated on biased data, for instance, might reinforce and magnify that bias. Therefore, it is essential to guarantee that AI systems are developed and put through testing to reduce bias and discrimination.

Cybersecurity: Hackers may utilize AI to find and take advantage of holes in computer systems, raising questions about cybersecurity. Hackers could employ AI algorithms to launch increasingly complex cyberattacks as AI technology advance. To prevent these attacks, it is necessary to update and enforce the legal frameworks for cybersecurity.

Governance: Since AI technologies have the potential to have substantial societal effects, including political and economic ramifications, there are concerns about how to oversee the creation and use of AI. This involves, among other things, concerns about data privacy, cybersecurity, and liability. It is crucial to make sure that AI technologies are created and implemented in a way that is consistent with societal values and ideals as they advance.

An overview of the legal implications of AI

New legal issues have arisen as a result of the development of artificial intelligence (AI), notably those relating to duty and accountability for the activities of autonomous systems. A summary of the legal ramifications of AI is provided below, along with relevant laws and rules:

Liability: AI systems are being employed more frequently in industries including healthcare, finance, and transportation as they become more advanced. This calls into question who is in charge of autonomous systems' actions. The existing legal system often places responsibility on the person or organization that caused the harm. However, because AI systems are autonomous, it might be challenging to assign blame for what they do. New laws and rules are therefore required to handle the problem of AI liability.

The General Data Protection Regulation (GDPR) of the European Union contains accountability clauses that mandate enterprises to assume accountability for the use of AI in decision-making procedures. The National Highway Traffic Safety Administration in the US has published rules on autonomous vehicles that spell out the duties of operators and manufacturers.

Intellectual property: AI is capable of producing original works of literature, music, and art. Another issue that needs to be resolved is the query of who owns these works. The author of a work is often regarded by existing laws as the owner of the copyright. However, it is uncertain who should be regarded as the creator in the case of AI-generated works.

The Copyright Office in the US has released guidance indicating that since AI-generated works are not produced by human authors, they are not protected by copyright. New rules and regulations are required to make it clear who owns works created by AI because the problem has not yet been resolved.

Privacy: AI systems frequently process a lot of sensitive personal information. Regulations and rules governing data protection must be followed when using this information. Examples of laws that control the use of personal data include the California Consumer Privacy Act (CCPA) in the United States and the General Data Protection Regulation (GDPR) in Europe.

Before collecting and using a person's personal information, companies are required by the GDPR to get that person's express consent. Individuals have the right to request that their data be destroyed and the right to know what personal information about them is being collected. Both statutes have provisions about data breaches, requiring businesses to notify the appropriate authorities of such breaches.

Discrimination: AI systems have the potential to reinforce biases and provide discriminatory results. The Civil Rights Act and the Americans with Disabilities Act forbid discrimination in the United States on the grounds of race, gender, and disability, among other protected classes. However, the use of AI is not particularly covered by these rules.

It is a requirement of the European Union's Ethics Guidelines for Trustworthy AI that AI systems not be biased towards certain people or groups. In accordance with the standards, AI systems should be open and accountable so that people may understand their judgments and question them.

Governments are starting to see the necessity for AI regulation. The Ethics Guidelines for Trustworthy AI, which provide a framework for the ethical development and deployment of AI, were introduced by the European Union in 2018. The rules place a strong emphasis on the value of openness, responsibility, and equality when using AI.

The National Artificial Intelligence Initiative Act was formed by the US in the same year to encourage the creation and ethical application of AI. The act has provisions for workforce development, national strategy, and research and development.

Driverless Vehicles: One area in particular where the legal ramifications of AI are particularly pertinent is the usage of driverless vehicles. The National Highway Traffic Safety Administration in the US has published rules on autonomous vehicles that spell out the duties of operators and manufacturers.

Before being allowed to operate on public roads in Europe, autonomous cars must adhere to the General Safety Regulation. The rule also contains liability clauses that demand that the one or parties responsible for the injury be held accountable.

Challenges and Potential Solutions for Regulating AI

Over the past few years, as the technology has advanced and proliferated, artificial intelligence (AI) has become more and more significant. There's no denying that AI has the potential to upend a variety of industries, but there are also concerns over bias, ethics, and responsibility. As a result, the regulation of AI has become a hot topic of debate, especially in industries where AI usage is increasing. In this post, we'll look at the problems with and potential solutions for AI regulation across different industries.

Healthcare: AI is frequently used in the healthcare industry to increase the accuracy of diagnoses, enhance patient outcomes, and automate tedious tasks. However, it's imperative to guarantee that AI is developed and used in an ethical and responsible manner. One of the key problems with AI legislation in the healthcare industry is protecting patient privacy and data. Healthcare organizations need to make sure AI algorithms are trained on enough data and that the data has been properly anonymized in order to protect patient privacy. Additionally, it's possible that the AI algorithms used in healthcare will be prejudiced, which could have an impact on how patients respond to treatment.

Creating a legislative framework requiring healthcare providers to reveal the data they use to train AI algorithms is one possible answer. This might comprise guidelines for the anonymization of data and objective assessments of AI systems to ensure their objectivity. Furthermore, the development of explainable AI (XAI) may lead to increased accountability and transparency in the use of AI in the healthcare industry.

The financial services industry is using AI to automate procedures like risk assessment and fraud detection. Despite the benefits, there is a potential that AI algorithms could continue to make biased lending decisions and create new types of financial risks.

One approach to finding solutions is to create a regulatory framework that compel financial firms to disclose their AI algorithms and how they are used in decision-making. Establishing oversight organizations to monitor the use of AI in banking and ensure that algorithms are examined for bias and inaccuracies may be necessary to achieve this. By using explainable AI, the lending process may become more transparent and accountable.

Transportation: As driverless vehicles proliferate, concerns about their safety and responsibility are expanding. Additionally, it's important to make sure that the AI algorithms used in transportation are clear and understandable in order to keep public trust.

One strategy is to establish legislative requirements for the creation and testing of autonomous vehicles, coupled with guidelines for data collection and safety testing. The disclosure of information regarding automakers' AI systems, such as how they learn and make decisions, may also be mandated by governments. The development of AI that is more understandable may also help to increase public trust in self-driving cars and make it easier for people to understand the decisions made by AI.

Production: Artificial intelligence (AI) is being used to automate a variety of production processes, including proactive maintenance and quality control. However, there is a possibility that AI algorithms will exercise bad judgment, leading to errors in production or equipment failure.

One solution is to establish legal requirements for the application of AI in manufacturing, coupled with guidelines for security measures and data protection. Governments can also request information from manufacturers about their AI algorithms, such as how they are trained and how decisions are made. The creation of explainable AI has the potential to improve both user confidence in these systems and human comprehension of AI judgements.

In order to effectively regulate AI in various industries, a careful balance must be struck between fostering innovation and upholding public trust. Governments, business executives, and other stakeholders must work together to develop legislative frameworks that encourage moral AI use while addressing the specific problems encountered by various economic sectors. The creation of explainable AI is essential for increasing responsibility, ensuring ethics, and ensuring that AI is used ethically and responsibly.

The Importance of Ethical Considerations in Legal Frameworks For AI.

The potential impact that AI systems could have on society is one of the main justifications for why ethical issues are significant in legal frameworks for AI. AI is becoming more and more incorporated into all facets of our lives as it develops, from healthcare to education to transportation and beyond. This indicates that AI systems have a tremendous potential to have an impact on society, both positively and negatively.

For instance, automating tasks with AI systems can result in higher productivity and efficiency. However, this may also lead to job losses and raise unemployment rates, which could have detrimental social and economic effects.

Furthermore, AI systems can affect how decisions are made in fields like recruiting, lending, and criminal justice. A lack of ethical design and implementation in AI systems can result in unfair outcomes for particular groups of people by reaffirming preexisting biases and discrimination.

AI systems can also be used for monitoring and surveillance, which has serious consequences for privacy and human liberties. AI systems can gather and analyze enormous amounts of personal data about people without their knowledge or agreement, which could potentially cause harm or lead to data misuse if they are not developed and implemented with privacy protections in mind.

Legal frameworks for AI must be created to make sure that AI systems operate in a way that is consistent with ethical principles and values in light of these potential effects. This calls for an all-encompassing strategy that takes into account many facets of AI development and deployment, such as data management and collecting, algorithm design and training, decision-making procedures, and accountability systems.

The creation of moral principles or code of conduct for developers is a crucial strategy for assuring ethical considerations in legal frameworks for AI. These rules can aid in ensuring that AI systems are created in a manner that is consistent with moral values like justice, accountability, and transparency.

Demanding accountability and openness in AI decision-making processes is another crucial strategy. This can entail creating AI systems that can explain decisions clearly and that can be developed, as well as creating channels for people to question and appeal decisions made by AI systems.

Legal frameworks for AI should also have clauses that prevent and lessen damage from AI systems. This could entail setting up legal frameworks to hold developers responsible for damage brought on by their AI systems, as well as requiring developers to do risk assessments and develop mitigation techniques.

To ensure that AI systems are created and used in a way that is consistent with societal values and beliefs, ethical issues are crucial in legal frameworks for AI. We can contribute to ensuring that AI technology is created and used in a responsible and ethical manner that benefits society as a whole by incorporating ethical issues into regulatory frameworks.

CHAPTER NINE

AI and Healthcare

Artificial intelligence (AI) has the potential to transform healthcare in numerous ways, such as improving patient outcomes, reducing costs, and increasing efficiency. However, it also raises several ethical concerns that must be addressed.

One of the primary ethical concerns surrounding AI in healthcare is privacy. The collection and use of patient data for AI applications raise questions about patient consent and the protection of personal information. Healthcare providers must ensure that patients are fully informed about how their data will be used and have the ability to control its use. Additionally, healthcare organizations must ensure that patient data is stored securely and used only for legitimate purposes.

Another ethical concern is bias in AI algorithms. AI systems are only as good as the data they are trained on, and if that data is biased, the resulting algorithms will also be biased. This can lead to discrimination against certain groups, such as racial or ethnic minorities, and result in inaccurate diagnoses or treatment recommendations. Healthcare organizations must be aware of these biases and take steps to mitigate them. For example, they may need to collect more diverse data or apply algorithms that counteract any inherent biases.

The use of AI in healthcare also raises questions about the impact on human relationships. While AI can provide valuable insights and support, it cannot replace the empathy and emotional support provided by human caregivers. Patients may feel uncomfortable sharing personal information with a machine, and may prefer to interact with a human doctor or nurse. Healthcare organizations must strike a balance between leveraging the benefits of AI and maintaining human connections with patients.

Additionally, the use of AI in healthcare raises questions about accountability and liability. If an AI system makes an incorrect diagnosis or treatment recommendation, who is responsible? Healthcare providers and organizations must ensure that they are accountable for the decisions made by AI systems and have processes in place to address any errors or issues that arise.

To address these ethical concerns, healthcare organizations must be transparent about how they use AI and ensure that patients are fully informed and engaged in the process. They must also ensure that AI algorithms are developed and trained in an ethical and responsible manner, and that they are regularly reviewed and updated to address any biases or inaccuracies. Finally, healthcare organizations must ensure that AI is used in conjunction with, and not as a replacement for, human caregivers. By taking these steps, healthcare providers can leverage the benefits of AI while maintaining ethical and responsible practices.

An overview of the current applications of AI in healthcare

Medical diagnosis and treatment are being improved by the use of artificial intelligence (AI) in healthcare. An overview of the current uses of AI in healthcare is provided below:

Medical imaging: One of the most prominent applications of AI in healthcare is medical imaging analysis. AI algorithms can analyze medical images, such as X-rays, CT scans, and MRIs, to detect and diagnose diseases. For instance, AI algorithms can analyze chest X-rays to identify potential lung diseases, such as pneumonia or tuberculosis. AI algorithms can also be trained to recognize patterns of breast cancer in mammograms, or to identify neurological conditions, such as Alzheimer's disease, in MRI scans. By automating the analysis of medical images, AI can provide faster and more accurate diagnoses, potentially saving lives.

Personalized medicine: Another application of AI in healthcare is personalized medicine. AI algorithms can analyze large amounts of patient data, such as genetics, medical history, and lifestyle factors, to develop personalized treatment plans. For example, AI can identify which treatments are most effective for specific patients, based on their individual characteristics, minimizing trial-and-error and improving patient outcomes. AI can also predict the likelihood of certain conditions, such as heart disease, based on a patient's medical history, lifestyle factors, and genetic profile, enabling healthcare providers to take proactive measures to prevent or manage the condition.

Drug discovery: AI is also being used to accelerate the drug discovery process. AI algorithms can analyze vast amounts of data, such as gene sequences, chemical structures, and clinical trial results, to identify potential drug candidates. By simulating the interactions between drugs and biological systems, AI can also predict how drugs will behave in the body, improving the accuracy and efficiency of drug development. Additionally, AI can help identify patients who are most likely to benefit from certain drugs, enabling personalized treatment plans.

Chronic disease management: AI is increasingly being used to monitor patients with chronic diseases, such as diabetes and heart disease, and provide personalized treatment recommendations. AI algorithms can analyze patient data, such as blood sugar levels and heart rate, and alert healthcare providers to potential issues. AI can also help patients manage their conditions by providing personalized recommendations on diet, exercise, and medication.

Medical chatbots: AI is also being used to develop medical chatbots, which can provide patients with personalized medical advice and support. Chatbots can answer patient questions, provide symptom assessments, and even schedule appointments with healthcare providers. Medical chatbots are particularly useful for patients who may not have easy access to healthcare providers or who may be hesitant to seek medical attention.

While the applications of AI in healthcare offer significant benefits, they also raise ethical concerns. Healthcare organizations must ensure that they are using AI in an ethical and responsible manner, while also leveraging its potential to improve patient outcomes. Additionally, AI should be used in conjunction with, and not as a replacement for, human caregivers. By taking these steps, healthcare providers can use AI to improve patient care and outcomes while maintaining ethical and responsible practices.

Examples of how AI is being used to improve patient outcomes and reduce healthcare costs

Artificial intelligence (AI) is being increasingly used in healthcare to improve patient outcomes and reduce healthcare costs. Here are some examples of how AI is being used in healthcare:

❖ **Early disease detection:** AI algorithms can analyze large amounts of patient data, such as medical history, lab results, and lifestyle factors, to identify early warning signs of diseases. By detecting diseases at an early stage, healthcare providers can intervene early, potentially preventing or delaying the progression of the disease. For instance, AI algorithms can analyze patient data to identify individuals at high risk for diabetes, enabling healthcare providers to recommend lifestyle changes or medication to prevent the onset of the disease.

❖ **Predictive analytics:** AI algorithms can predict which patients are at risk of developing certain conditions or complications, enabling healthcare providers to take proactive measures to prevent or manage the condition. For example, AI algorithms can analyze patient data to predict which patients are at high risk for hospital readmissions, enabling healthcare providers to provide targeted interventions to prevent readmissions.

❖ **Personalized treatment plans:** AI algorithms can analyze patient data, such as genetics, medical history, and lifestyle factors, to develop personalized treatment plans.

❖ **Medical image analysis:** AI algorithms can analyze medical images, such as X-rays, CT scans, and MRIs, to detect and diagnose diseases. By automating the analysis of medical images, AI can provide faster and more accurate diagnoses, potentially saving lives. For example, AI algorithms can analyze chest X-rays to identify potential lung diseases, such as pneumonia or tuberculosis. AI can also be trained to recognize patterns of breast cancer in mammograms, or to identify neurological conditions, such as Alzheimer's disease, in MRI scans.

❖ **Chronic disease management:** AI is being used to monitor patients with chronic diseases, such as diabetes and heart disease, and provide personalized treatment recommendations. By analyzing patient data, such as blood sugar levels and heart rate, AI can alert healthcare providers to potential issues and help patients manage their conditions by providing personalized recommendations on diet, exercise, and medication. This can reduce hospitalizations and emergency room visits, lowering healthcare costs.

❖ **Medical chatbots:** AI-powered medical chatbots can provide patients with personalized medical advice and support, reducing the need for costly in-person consultations. Chatbots can answer patient questions, provide symptom assessments, and even schedule appointments with healthcare providers. Medical chatbots are particularly useful for patients who may not have easy access to healthcare providers or who may be hesitant to seek medical attention.

❖ **Virtual assistants for healthcare providers:** AI-powered virtual assistants can help healthcare providers streamline administrative tasks, such as scheduling appointments, updating medical records, and billing. By automating these tasks, healthcare providers can focus on patient care, potentially reducing the need for additional staff and lowering healthcare costs.

❖ **Drug discovery:** AI is being used to accelerate the drug discovery process by identifying potential drug candidates and predicting their efficacy and safety. By analyzing large amounts of data, such as gene expression and protein interactions, AI can identify potential drug targets and predict the effectiveness of drugs in treating certain diseases. This can help to reduce the time and cost of developing new drugs, and potentially improve patient outcomes.

❖ **Robotic surgery:** AI-powered surgical robots are being used to perform minimally invasive surgeries with greater precision and accuracy than human surgeons. These robots use advanced imaging and sensing technologies to provide real-time feedback to surgeons, enabling them to perform complex surgeries with greater safety and efficiency. By reducing the risk of complications and shortening recovery times, robotic surgery can lower healthcare costs and improve patient outcomes.

❖ **Remote patient monitoring:** AI is being used to monitor patients remotely, enabling healthcare providers to monitor patients outside of the hospital or clinic setting. By analyzing patient data, such as vital signs and medication adherence, AI can alert healthcare providers to potential issues and provide real-time recommendations for treatment. This can reduce hospital readmissions and emergency room visits, and potentially improve patient outcomes.

❖ **Mental health care:** AI is being used to improve the diagnosis and treatment of mental health disorders, such as depression and anxiety. By analyzing patient data, such as social media activity and speech patterns, AI can identify potential mental health issues and provide personalized treatment recommendations. This can help to reduce the stigma associated with mental health disorders and improve patient outcomes.

❖ **Predictive maintenance:** AI is being used to monitor medical equipment and predict when maintenance is needed, reducing downtime and the need for costly repairs. By analyzing data from medical equipment, such as CT scanners and MRI machines, AI can identify potential issues before they become major problems, enabling healthcare providers to schedule maintenance and repairs at the most convenient times.

❖ **Patient engagement:** AI-powered chatbots and virtual assistants can be used to engage patients in their healthcare by providing personalized health advice, reminders, and motivation. This can help patients to adhere to treatment plans and make lifestyle changes that improve their health outcomes.

❖ **Clinical trials:** AI is being used to improve the design and execution of clinical trials, enabling researchers to more efficiently test the safety and efficacy of new drugs and treatments. By analyzing patient data and predicting outcomes, AI can help to reduce the cost and time required to bring new drugs to market.

Overall, the use of AI in healthcare has the potential to revolutionize patient care and improve health outcomes while reducing healthcare costs. However, it is important to ensure that the development and deployment of AI in healthcare is carefully regulated to ensure patient safety and privacy.

The Ethical Implications and Challenges Of Using AI In Healthcare

Accountability and liability: As AI systems get more complicated, it might be challenging to pinpoint who is in charge of making decisions that the system makes. This may lead to questions about responsibility and culpability, particularly if a patient is harmed as a result of a system malfunction. In order to ensure that responsibility and culpability are appropriately distributed, it is crucial to have clear norms and regulations around the use of AI in healthcare.

Patient autonomy: While AI systems can be used to prescribe treatments based on a wealth of data, patients may have unique preferences and needs that are not reflected in the data. Concerns concerning patient autonomy and the possibility of patients being led toward therapies that may not be consistent with their values may arise as a result of this. It's critical to guarantee that patients have the autonomy to make their own healthcare decisions and that patients' autonomy is taken into account when developing AI systems.

Unforeseen effects: The application of AI in healthcare may lead to unforeseen outcomes like over-reliance on the technology or the emergence of new health inequities. It's crucial to perform in-depth analyses of the potential hazards and advantages of AI systems and to continuously monitor their use to make sure that any unintended repercussions are found and dealt with.

Obtaining a lot of patient data is necessary for the application of AI in healthcare, which raises questions about informed permission. Patients might not be entirely aware of how their information is being utilized or they might not be aware of the possible dangers of AI systems. Before utilizing AI systems in healthcare, it's crucial to make sure that patients are fully informed about how their data is being used and to gain their informed consent.

Fairness and justice: While AI systems are capable of forecasting health outcomes and recommending treatments, it is possible that these forecasts will be influenced by social and economic issues that are unrelated to a patient's health. As some patients might receive less favorable treatment suggestions or be barred from specific treatments due to circumstances beyond their control, this might raise questions about fairness and justice in healthcare. It's crucial to create fair and equitable AI systems and make sure that racial, gender, and socioeconomic considerations have no impact on healthcare decisions.

CHAPTER TEN

AI and Education

Personalized learning opportunities, effective grading and feedback, and adaptive exams are just a few of the advantages that AI is bringing to education. Particularly, AI-driven personalized learning solutions can deliver individualized learning experiences that are catered to each student's unique learning preferences, background, and skills. AI can forecast student requirements by evaluating student data, identifying patterns, and providing individualized training and feedback that boost engagement and results.

Another effective application of AI in education is adaptive testing. These tests adjust in real-time to how well the learner is performing, offering more or less difficult material accordingly. This strategy aids in ensuring that each student is appropriately challenged, which improves learning results and decreases dissatisfaction or boredom.

AI can help simplify feedback and grading, lightening the strain on teachers and allowing them more time for individualized education. Multiple choice and fill-in-the-blank questions can be handled by automated grading systems, freeing teachers to concentrate on more complex activities like writing comments and one-on-one student help.

AI-powered virtual instructors are another fascinating new development in education. By responding to inquiries, offering feedback, and supplying targeted support when and where it's needed, these virtual assistants may offer students support and direction on demand.

In addition, there are difficulties and ethical issues related to the application of AI in education. Bias is one of the main issues. If the data used to train AI systems is biased or lacking, it can amplify those biases and continue to treat some kids unfairly and maintain existing imbalances. This emphasizes the significance of utilizing a range of representative datasets when training AI systems, as well as the necessity of identifying and eliminating algorithmic biases.

Data security and privacy are additional issues. Large amounts of student data are needed for AI systems, so it's crucial to make sure that this data is shielded from misuse and illegal access. To enable the appropriate use of AI in education, strong data privacy and security measures, such as encryption, secure storage, and user consent, are essential.

When using AI in education, transparency and comprehensibility are also important factors to take into account. It might be challenging to comprehend how AI systems make judgments as they become increasingly complicated. This can make it difficult for teachers to justify choices to children and can cause issues with responsibility and culpability. For fostering trust and confidence in their use, AI systems must be clear and understandable.

Another issue with AI in education is dependence on technology. Although AI has the potential to be a tremendous tool for enhancing education, it cannot take the place of human teachers. Overreliance on technology may lead to a reduction in significant social and emotional contacts, which are crucial for growth and learning. It's crucial to strike a balance between employing artificial intelligence (AI) to improve and augment education and maintaining the crucial function of human educators.

Finally, when AI develops the capacity to carry out functions once handled by human instructors, there is a risk of job displacement. It's critical to take into account how AI will affect the education workforce and to establish plans to retrain and upskill employees in impacted professions.

An overview of the current and potential applications of AI in education

Personalized Learning: One of the biggest advantages of AI in education is its ability to personalize learning. With AI-powered algorithms, educators can analyze student data such as performance history, interests, and learning styles to develop tailored learning plans. These plans can then be implemented through adaptive learning platforms that adjust the pace and difficulty of lessons to match each student's abilities. This personalized approach to learning has been shown to increase student engagement, motivation, and achievement.

Adaptive Assessments: Traditional assessments are often static, providing the same set of questions to all students regardless of their ability level. However, AI-powered adaptive assessments can adjust the difficulty of questions in real-time based on each student's answers, ensuring that each student is challenged at an appropriate level. This type of assessment provides a more accurate measure of student understanding and allows teachers to identify learning gaps more efficiently.

Grading and Feedback: AI-powered grading and feedback systems can reduce the time and effort required for manual grading tasks. For example, multiple-choice and short answer questions can be graded automatically, freeing up teachers to focus on more complex tasks such as providing feedback and support to students. Additionally, AI can provide more consistent and objective grading, reducing the potential for grading bias.

Virtual Tutors: AI-powered virtual tutors are becoming increasingly popular in education. These systems can provide on-demand support to students, answering questions and providing feedback as needed. They can also monitor student progress and provide targeted support to students who are struggling. This type of support can be especially valuable in online or blended learning environments, where students may not have access to a teacher or tutor in person.

Curriculum Design: AI can help teachers design more effective and engaging curriculum. By analyzing student data, AI can identify areas where students are struggling and recommend content and resources that are best suited to each student's needs. This can lead to more efficient and effective teaching, improving student outcomes and reducing teacher workload.

Educational Research: AI can play an important role in educational research. By analyzing large datasets, AI can identify patterns and relationships that may not be immediately apparent to human researchers. This can lead to new insights and discoveries that can inform educational policy and practice.

Language Learning: AI-powered language learning systems are becoming increasingly popular in education. These systems can provide personalized instruction and feedback that help students improve their language skills. They can analyze student pronunciation and grammar, provide real-time feedback, and adapt instruction to each student's individual needs.

Special Education: AI can be especially valuable in special education. For example, speech recognition systems can help students with speech and language disorders, while text-to-speech systems can read text aloud to students with visual impairments. Additionally, AI-powered assistive technologies can help students with disabilities to participate more fully in the classroom.

While the potential benefits of AI in education are clear, there are also potential risks and challenges to consider. For example, there are concerns about the potential for AI to reinforce existing biases or perpetuate inequalities. Additionally, there is a risk that reliance on AI-powered systems could reduce the role of teachers in education. As such, it is important to approach the use of AI in education with caution and to prioritize ethical considerations. Ultimately, the responsible and ethical use of AI has the potential to improve education outcomes for all students.

How AI Is Being Used to Improve Student Outcomes and Reduce Achievement Gaps

There are many examples of how AI is being used to improve student outcomes and reduce achievement gaps in education. Here are some examples:

1. **Intelligent Tutoring Systems:** Intelligent tutoring systems (ITS) are a type of AI technology that provide personalized support to students. These systems use machine learning algorithms to analyze student data and provide real-time feedback and guidance. ITS have been shown to improve student achievement, particularly for students who are struggling.

2. **Adaptive Learning Platforms:** Adaptive learning platforms use AI algorithms to provide personalized learning experiences to students. These platforms analyze student data, such as performance history and learning style, to create individualized learning plans that adjust the pace and difficulty of content to match each student's needs. These platforms have been

shown to improve student outcomes and reduce achievement gaps.

3. **Automated Grading and Feedback:** Automated grading and feedback systems use AI algorithms to grade assignments and provide feedback to students. These systems can reduce the time and effort required for manual grading tasks and provide more consistent and objective grading. This can help reduce achievement gaps by ensuring that all students receive fair and accurate grading.

4. **Natural Language Processing:** Natural language processing (NLP) is a type of AI technology that can analyze and understand human language. NLP can be used in education to analyze student writing and provide feedback on grammar and syntax. This can be particularly valuable for students who are learning English as a second language.

5. **Predictive Analytics:** Predictive analytics use AI algorithms to analyze student data and predict future outcomes, such as graduation rates or performance on standardized tests. This can help educators identify students who may be at risk of falling behind and provide targeted support to help them succeed.

6. **Digital Assistants:** Digital assistants, such as chatbots or voice assistants, use AI technology to provide on-demand support to students. These assistants can answer questions, provide feedback, and offer guidance on assignments. This can be particularly valuable for students who are learning remotely or who may not have access to a teacher or tutor in person.

7. **Personalized Curriculum:** AI can be used to create personalized curriculum for students based on their individual needs and interests. For example, AI algorithms can analyze student data to identify areas

where students are struggling and recommend content and resources that are best suited to each student's needs. This can help reduce achievement gaps by ensuring that all students have access to high-quality, personalized instruction.

Overall, AI has the potential to revolutionize education by providing personalized support to students and reducing achievement gaps. However, it is important to approach the use of AI in education with caution and to prioritize ethical considerations. Ultimately, the responsible and ethical use of AI has the potential to improve education outcomes for all students.

The Ethical Implications and Challenges of Using AI in Education

The use of AI in education presents many ethical implications and challenges that must be considered. Here are some of the key concerns:

1. **Data privacy:** The use of AI in education requires the collection and analysis of student data. It is important to ensure that this data is collected and stored securely, and that student privacy is protected. Educators and policymakers must be transparent about the types of data that are being collected and how they will be used.
2. **Algorithmic bias:** AI algorithms can be biased if they are trained on biased data. This can lead to unequal treatment of students and reinforce existing inequities. It is important to ensure that AI algorithms are designed and trained in a way that is unbiased and equitable.
3. **Transparency:** AI algorithms can be difficult to understand, even for experts. It is important to ensure that the use of AI in education is transparent, so that

educators and students understand how decisions are being made.

4. **Autonomy:** The use of AI in education raises questions about student autonomy. Students may feel like they are being tracked and monitored by AI systems, which could lead to feelings of anxiety and stress. It is important to ensure that students have agency in their own learning and that the use of AI does not infringe on their autonomy.

5. **Accountability:** It can be difficult to assign responsibility when something goes wrong with an AI system. It is important to ensure that there is accountability for the use of AI in education, so that educators and policymakers can be held responsible for the decisions that are made.

6. **Human interaction:** The use of AI in education raises questions about the role of human interaction in learning. While AI can provide personalized support and feedback, it cannot replace the value of human interaction in learning. It is important to ensure that the use of AI does not replace human interaction in education.

7. **Equitable access:** The use of AI in education has the potential to exacerbate existing inequities if not implemented carefully. It is important to ensure that all students have equitable access to AI-powered tools and resources, and that the use of AI does not further disadvantage marginalized communities.

8. **Accountability for decisions:** AI systems can make decisions that impact students, such as determining which resources or courses to recommend. It is

important to ensure that these decisions are transparent, explainable, and accountable.

9. **Teacher training:** The use of AI in education requires teachers to have a certain level of digital literacy and data literacy. It is important to ensure that teachers are properly trained to use AI systems in the classroom, and that they have the skills to interpret and act on the data generated by these systems.

10. **Impact on teaching practices:** The use of AI in education can change the way that teachers teach. Teachers may rely more heavily on AI-generated data, and may spend less time engaging with students. It is important to ensure that the use of AI in education does not replace or undermine traditional teaching practices.

11. **Dependence on technology:** The use of AI in education can create a dependency on technology. This can be problematic if the technology fails or if students do not have access to it. It is important to ensure that the use of AI in education is not overly reliant on technology, and that alternative methods of instruction are available.

12. **Lack of student agency:** The use of AI in education can limit student agency and autonomy. Students may feel like they are being directed by AI systems, rather than being able to make their own decisions about their learning. It is important to ensure that the use of AI in education does not undermine student agency and autonomy.

13. **Unintended consequences:** The use of AI in education can have unintended consequences. For example, AI systems may identify patterns in student

data that reinforce existing biases or stereotypes. It is important to ensure that the use of AI in education is constantly monitored and evaluated, so that any unintended consequences can be identified and addressed.

In order to address these ethical implications and challenges, it is important for educators, policymakers, and technologists to work together. They must engage in ongoing discussions about the use of AI in education, and work to develop policies and practices that prioritize student privacy, equity, and autonomy. By doing so, they can ensure that the use of AI in education is responsible, ethical, and effective.

CHAPTER ELEVEN

AI and the Environment

AI has the potential to play a transformative role in addressing environmental challenges. From climate change and conservation to energy management and waste reduction, AI offers a range of solutions that can help us create a more sustainable future. Let's take a closer look at some of the specific ways in which AI is being used in environmental applications:

Climate modeling: One of the most promising applications of AI in environmental science is in climate modeling. Researchers are using machine learning to analyze vast amounts of data on climate patterns, including historical weather data, satellite imagery, and ocean temperature data. By analyzing this data, AI systems can identify patterns and make more accurate predictions about future climate trends. This information can help policymakers develop more effective climate mitigation and adaptation strategies.

Energy management: Another important application of AI in the environment is in energy management. AI systems can analyze data on energy consumption to identify areas of inefficiency and suggest ways to reduce waste. For example, an AI system can analyze data from smart meters to identify buildings or homes that are using more energy than necessary. It can also suggest ways to optimize energy use, such as adjusting temperature settings or using more energy-efficient appliances.

Conservation: AI can also be used to monitor and protect endangered species and their habitats. AI-powered cameras can be used to identify individual animals and track their movements over time. This information can be used to develop more effective conservation strategies, such as identifying areas that are critical to the survival of a particular species.

Agriculture: AI can help optimize crop yields and reduce the use of pesticides and other inputs. By analyzing data on soil quality, weather patterns, and other factors, AI systems can make recommendations on planting and harvesting schedules, as well as suggest ways to reduce the use of pesticides and other chemicals. This can help farmers increase their yields while also reducing their impact on the environment.

Waste management: Finally, AI can be used to improve waste management by analyzing patterns in waste generation and identifying opportunities for recycling and reuse. For example, an AI system can analyze data on waste generation and suggest ways to reduce waste, such as by implementing more efficient recycling programs or encouraging people to use reusable containers.

While the use of AI in environmental applications offers many potential benefits, there are also ethical and social implications that need to be considered. Here are some examples:

Bias: One of the biggest challenges in using AI in environmental applications is bias. AI systems are only as good as the data they are trained on. If the data is biased, the AI system will also be biased. For example, if an AI system is used to identify endangered species, it may not be able to recognize species that are not well represented in the training data.

Privacy: The use of AI to monitor and track environmental data can raise concerns about privacy. For example, if AI-powered cameras are used to monitor wildlife, there may be concerns about the collection and use of sensitive data.

Automation: The use of AI in environmental applications may lead to job losses in some areas, such as manual wildlife monitoring or waste management. It is important to consider the potential social and economic impacts of these changes.

Unintended consequences: As with any technology, the use of AI in environmental applications can have unintended consequences. For example, if an AI system is used to optimize energy use, it may inadvertently increase energy consumption in other areas.

Dependence on technology: The use of AI in environmental applications can create a dependence on technology. This can be problematic if the technology fails or if there are disruptions in the data or power supply.

An Overview of The Current And Potential Applications of AI in Environmental Management

Artificial intelligence (AI) has the potential to revolutionize the way we manage and protect the environment. From identifying endangered species and tracking their movements to predicting natural disasters, AI has a wide range of applications in environmental management. Here are some of the key ways in which AI is being used and has the potential to be used in environmental management:

Conservation: One of the most important applications of AI in environmental management is in conservation efforts. AI can help monitor and protect endangered species and their habitats. For example, AI-powered cameras can be used to identify individual animals and track their movements over time. This information can be used to develop more effective conservation strategies, such as identifying areas that are critical to the survival of a particular species. AI systems are also being used to detect illegal poaching and deforestation, allowing authorities to take action to protect wildlife.

Pollution control: Another important application of AI in environmental management is in pollution control. AI can be used to monitor and control pollution levels in a variety of environments, including air, water, and soil. By analyzing data from sensors, AI can detect patterns and identify sources of pollution, allowing authorities to take action to address the problem. For example, AI systems are being used to detect pollution levels in waterways and to identify areas of high pollution in urban environments.

Climate change: AI has enormous potential in the fight against climate change. By analyzing large amounts of data on climate patterns, including historical weather data, satellite imagery, and ocean temperature data, AI systems can identify patterns and make more accurate predictions about future climate trends. This information can help policymakers develop more effective climate mitigation and adaptation strategies. For example, AI can be used to optimize renewable energy production by predicting weather patterns and adjusting energy production accordingly.

Waste management: AI can also be used to optimize waste management processes by analyzing patterns in waste generation and identifying opportunities for recycling and reuse. For example, an AI system can analyze data on waste generation and suggest ways to reduce waste, such as by implementing more efficient recycling programs or encouraging people to use reusable containers. AI can also be used to optimize waste collection routes, reducing emissions and improving efficiency.

Energy management: AI can be used to optimize energy use and reduce greenhouse gas emissions. By analyzing data on energy consumption, AI systems can identify areas of inefficiency and suggest ways to reduce waste. For example, an AI system can analyze data from smart meters to identify buildings or homes that are using more energy than necessary. It can also suggest ways to optimize energy use, such as adjusting temperature settings or using more energy-efficient appliances.

Natural disaster prediction and response: AI can be used to predict natural disasters such as floods and wildfires, allowing authorities to take action to protect people and property. For example, AI can be used to analyze satellite imagery to identify areas at risk of flooding and to develop evacuation plans. AI can also be used to predict the spread of wildfires and to identify the most effective firefighting strategies.

Despite the enormous potential benefits of AI in environmental management, there are also ethical and social implications that need to be considered. For example, the use of AI to monitor and track environmental data can raise concerns about privacy. Additionally, the automation of tasks in environmental management may lead to job losses in some areas. It is important to consider the potential social and economic impacts of these changes and to work towards solutions that benefit both the environment and society.

How AI Is Being Used to Improve Environmental Outcomes and Sustainability

Artificial Intelligence (AI) is being used to improve environmental outcomes and sustainability in a wide range of applications. Here are some examples of how AI is being used to achieve these goals:

Renewable energy: AI is being used to optimize the production and distribution of renewable energy. By analyzing data on energy production and consumption, AI systems can identify patterns and make more accurate predictions about future energy needs. This information can be used to optimize the use of renewable energy sources such as wind and solar power, reducing reliance on fossil fuels and reducing greenhouse gas emissions.

Precision agriculture: AI is being used to improve the efficiency and sustainability of agricultural practices. By analyzing data on soil quality, weather patterns, and crop yields, AI systems can help farmers make more informed decisions about when to plant, water, and harvest crops. This information can help reduce waste, improve yields, and reduce the use of fertilizers and pesticides.

Water management: AI is being used to optimize water management practices, improving efficiency and reducing waste. For example, AI systems can analyze data on water usage patterns and identify areas of inefficiency. This information can be used to develop more efficient water management strategies, such as reducing leaks or implementing more effective irrigation systems.

Waste management: AI is being used to optimize waste management practices, improving efficiency and reducing waste. By analyzing data on waste generation and disposal, AI systems can help identify opportunities for recycling and reuse. This information can be used to develop more efficient waste management strategies, reducing the amount of waste sent to landfills and promoting the use of recycled materials.

Smart cities: AI is being used to improve the sustainability of urban environments. By analyzing data on traffic patterns, energy usage, and waste generation, AI systems can help cities develop more efficient and sustainable infrastructure. For example, AI systems can optimize traffic flow, reducing congestion and emissions, or identify areas of high pollution and implement strategies to improve air quality.

Conservation: AI is being used to monitor and protect endangered species and their habitats, improving conservation efforts. For example, AI-powered cameras can be used to identify individual animals and track their movements over time. This information can be used to develop more effective conservation strategies, such as identifying areas that are critical to the survival of a particular species. AI systems are also being used to detect illegal poaching and deforestation, allowing authorities to take action to protect wildlife.

Ocean conservation: AI is being used to monitor and protect marine environments, improving conservation efforts. For example, AI-powered underwater drones can be used to detect and map coral reefs, identifying areas that are at risk of degradation or destruction. AI systems can also be used to monitor ocean temperatures and currents, helping scientists understand the impact of climate change on marine ecosystems.

Air quality: AI is being used to monitor and improve air quality in urban environments. By analyzing data on emissions and weather patterns, AI systems can identify areas of high pollution and develop strategies to improve air quality. For example, AI-powered air purifiers can be used to remove pollutants from the air in specific areas, while smart traffic management systems can be used to reduce emissions from vehicles.

Disaster response: AI is being used to improve disaster response efforts, helping communities to prepare for and respond to natural disasters such as hurricanes, floods, and wildfires. By analyzing data on weather patterns and natural disasters, AI systems can help predict the likelihood and severity of future disasters, allowing authorities to take preventative action. AI can also be used to help coordinate emergency responses, identifying areas that need the most assistance and directing resources where they are most needed.

Sustainable supply chains: AI is being used to improve the sustainability of supply chains, reducing the environmental impact of products and services. By analyzing data on production processes and supply chain logistics, AI systems can identify areas of inefficiency and waste. This information can be used to develop more sustainable practices, such as reducing the use of single-use plastics or improving the energy efficiency of production facilities.

Despite the many benefits of using AI in environmental management and conservation, there are also ethical implications and challenges to consider. For example, there is a risk that AI could be used to justify environmentally harmful practices, such as increased resource extraction or pollution, by claiming that they are necessary to support AI systems. Additionally, there is a risk that AI systems could perpetuate biases and inequalities, such as by favoring certain communities or industries over others in environmental decision-making processes.

To address these challenges, it is important to ensure that AI systems are designed and implemented with ethical considerations in mind. This includes ensuring that data used in AI systems is accurate, unbiased, and representative of all communities and perspectives. It also includes ensuring that AI systems are transparent and accountable, allowing for meaningful public participation in environmental decision-making processes.

The Ethical Implications and Challenges of Using AI in Environmental Management

While AI has the potential to greatly improve environmental management and conservation efforts, it also raises a number of ethical concerns and challenges. Here are some of the most significant ethical implications and challenges of using AI in environmental management:

Bias and fairness: AI systems are only as good as the data they are trained on, and this data can be biased or incomplete. If an AI system is trained on data that reflects existing biases or inequalities, it may perpetuate or even amplify these biases. This could lead to unfair or inequitable outcomes in environmental management and conservation efforts.

Privacy and security: The use of AI in environmental management and conservation may involve the collection and analysis of large amounts of data, including personal data. This raises concerns about privacy and data security, particularly if the data is shared with third parties or used for other purposes beyond environmental management.

Accountability and transparency: AI systems can be complex and opaque, making it difficult to understand how they work and how decisions are made. This lack of transparency can make it difficult to hold AI systems accountable for their actions, particularly in cases where they make decisions that have significant environmental impacts.

Dependence and autonomy: There is a risk that the use of AI in environmental management could lead to a dependence on technology, reducing human autonomy and agency in decision-making. This could be particularly problematic if AI systems are used to make decisions that have significant environmental impacts, without appropriate human oversight.

Unintended consequences: The use of AI in environmental management and conservation could have unintended consequences, particularly if AI systems are not properly designed or tested. For example, an AI system designed to optimize energy efficiency could end up creating new environmental problems, such as increased greenhouse gas emissions.

To address these ethical implications and challenges, it is important to ensure that AI systems are designed and implemented with ethics in mind. This includes ensuring that data used in AI systems is accurate, unbiased, and representative of all communities and perspectives. It also includes ensuring that AI systems are transparent and accountable, allowing for meaningful public participation in environmental decision-making processes.

In addition, it is important to recognize the limitations of AI and to ensure that humans remain in control of environmental management and conservation efforts. This means using AI to support human decision-making, rather than replacing it entirely. It also means recognizing that AI is not a silver bullet, and that it should be used in conjunction with other approaches to environmental management and conservation.

CHAPTER TWELVE

AI and the Future of Work

The increasing use of AI is rapidly changing the nature of work in many industries, from healthcare to finance to manufacturing. As AI becomes more advanced and sophisticated, it has the potential to automate more and more tasks, from basic data entry to complex decision-making.

One of the key benefits of AI in the future of work is the ability to automate repetitive and mundane tasks, freeing up workers to focus on more complex and creative tasks that require human judgement and decision-making. For example, in the healthcare industry, AI is being used to automate routine administrative tasks, such as appointment scheduling and medical record keeping, so that healthcare professionals can spend more time providing patient care.

Another potential application of AI in the future of work is the use of predictive analytics to identify skills gaps and develop training programs that can help workers develop the skills they need to succeed in new roles. This could help to reduce skills mismatches and ensure that workers are better prepared for the jobs of the future.

In addition to automating tasks and improving workforce development, AI can also be used to improve the efficiency and effectiveness of business processes. For example, in the finance industry, AI is being used to analyze large amounts of data to identify fraud and other financial crimes, which can help to reduce risk and protect the financial system.

However, there are also concerns about the impact of AI on the workforce. One concern is that AI could lead to job displacement and result in a significant number of workers being left behind. For example, many jobs in manufacturing, retail, and transportation are at risk of being automated.

To address this issue, it will be important to invest in retraining programs and support for workers who are affected by automation. This could include programs that help workers transition to new jobs or retrain for new roles in emerging industries.

Another concern is that the use of AI in hiring and employment decisions could exacerbate existing biases and discrimination. For example, if AI algorithms are trained on historical data that reflects bias against certain groups, then the algorithms themselves may perpetuate this bias.

To address this issue, it will be important to ensure that AI systems used in employment decisions are designed and tested to be fair and unbiased. This could include conducting regular audits and reviews of AI systems to ensure that they are not perpetuating bias.

In addition to these concerns, there are also ethical implications related to the use of AI in the future of work. For example, there is a risk that the use of AI could lead to the creation of a two-tiered workforce, where a small number of highly skilled workers benefit from the increased efficiency and productivity that AI brings, while the majority of workers are left with low-skilled jobs and limited opportunities for advancement.

To address these ethical concerns, it will be important to ensure that the benefits of AI are shared fairly across the workforce. This could include policies that promote the development of high-skilled jobs and ensure that workers are paid a fair wage for their work.

Furthermore, it is important to note that the use of AI in the future of work will not be a panacea for all problems. It will be important to recognize the limitations of AI and to ensure that it is used in a way that complements human skills and expertise, rather than replacing them.

An overview of the current and potential impact of AI on the job market

Artificial intelligence (AI) has been touted as a game changer in the world of work, with the potential to automate tasks, increase productivity, and enhance decision making. However, there are concerns about the impact of AI on the job market and the potential for job displacement, particularly for low-skilled workers.

Current applications of AI in the job market include automating routine tasks such as data entry, customer service, and transportation, as well as enhancing decision making through machine learning algorithms. In addition, AI is being used to augment human abilities in areas such as healthcare, finance, and education.

Despite the potential benefits of AI in the job market, there are concerns about job displacement, particularly for low-skilled workers. According to a 2018 report by the McKinsey Global Institute, up to 375 million workers, or about 14% of the global workforce, may need to switch occupations or acquire new skills by 2030 due to automation and other technological advances.

However, there are also potential benefits of AI for the job market, such as the creation of new jobs in fields related to AI development, maintenance, and integration, as well as the potential for increased productivity and economic growth.

In addition, there is the potential for AI to enhance the quality of work by automating routine and mundane tasks, allowing workers to focus on more creative and engaging work. AI can also be used to provide personalized training and professional development opportunities to workers, helping them to acquire new skills and adapt to changing job requirements.

There are also concerns about the ethical implications of AI in the job market, particularly with regard to bias and discrimination. AI algorithms may inadvertently perpetuate biases based on factors such as race, gender, and age, leading to unfair hiring practices and unequal treatment in the workplace.

To address these concerns, there is a need for transparency and accountability in the development and implementation of AI systems in the job market. This includes ensuring that AI algorithms are developed using diverse data sets and are regularly audited for bias and discrimination.

How AI Is Being Used To Augment And Improve Human Work

AI is transforming the way we work in a variety of industries, and its impact is both positive and negative. While there are concerns about the potential displacement of jobs, there are also many examples of how AI is being used to augment and improve human work.

One area where AI is being used to augment human work is in healthcare. AI is being used to improve patient care by augmenting the work of healthcare professionals. For example, AI can be used to analyze medical images and help diagnose diseases, allowing doctors to make more accurate diagnoses and provide more targeted treatment. AI can also be used to monitor patient data in real-time, alerting healthcare providers to potential health issues before they become serious. Additionally, AI is being used to improve the efficiency of healthcare operations by automating administrative tasks, such as scheduling appointments and processing insurance claims.

Another area where AI is being used to augment human work is in manufacturing. AI is being used to improve productivity and efficiency in manufacturing by augmenting the work of human workers. For example, AI-powered robots can work alongside human workers to perform repetitive or dangerous tasks, such as lifting heavy objects or working in hazardous environments. This allows human workers to focus on more complex tasks that require creativity and problem-solving skills. Additionally, AI can be used to optimize manufacturing processes, reducing waste and improving the overall quality of products.

In finance, AI is being used to improve financial decision making by augmenting the work of financial analysts and traders. For example, AI algorithms can analyze large amounts of financial data in real-time, allowing traders to make more informed investment decisions. AI can also be used to detect fraudulent activity and prevent financial crime. Additionally, AI is being used to improve customer service by automating routine tasks, such as answering common questions and resolving simple issues.

In education, AI is being used to improve education by augmenting the work of teachers and education professionals. For example, AI-powered tutoring systems can provide personalized learning experiences for students, helping them to learn at their own pace and address areas of weakness. AI can also be used to analyze student data and provide teachers with insights into student performance, allowing them to provide targeted interventions and support. Additionally, AI is being used to automate administrative tasks, such as grading papers and tracking attendance, allowing teachers to focus on teaching and student engagement.

Finally, in agriculture, AI is being used to improve crop yields and reduce waste by augmenting the work of farmers. For example, AI-powered drones can be used to monitor crop health and detect pest infestations, allowing farmers to take targeted action to protect their crops. AI can also be used to analyze weather patterns and predict crop yields, helping farmers to make more informed decisions about planting and harvesting. Additionally, AI is being used to automate routine tasks, such as watering and fertilizing crops, freeing up farmers to focus on more complex tasks that require human expertise.

While these examples demonstrate the potential benefits of AI in augmenting human work, there are also ethical and social implications that need to be considered. For example, there is concern that AI may reinforce existing biases and exacerbate inequality. Additionally, there are concerns about the privacy and security of personal data, as well as the potential for AI to be used for harmful purposes. As such, it is important to carefully consider the ethical implications of AI in the workplace, and to implement appropriate safeguards to protect individuals and society as a whole.

The Ethical Implications And Challenges Of Using AI In The Workplace

The growing adoption of AI in the workplace has raised many ethical concerns and challenges. Here are some of the key ethical implications and challenges of using AI in the workplace:

Job displacement: One of the biggest ethical concerns around AI in the workplace is the displacement of human workers. AI-powered automation can replace human workers in many jobs, leading to job losses and economic disruption. This can have significant social and ethical implications, particularly in industries where large numbers of workers are at risk of being displaced.

Bias and discrimination: AI systems are only as unbiased as the data they are trained on, and if this data contains biases, it can result in discriminatory outcomes. This is particularly concerning when it comes to hiring and promotion decisions, as biased AI systems could perpetuate discrimination and bias against certain groups of people.

Invasion of privacy: AI systems can collect and analyze vast amounts of data on employees, including their behavior, preferences, and even their emotions. This raises concerns around privacy and surveillance, particularly if this data is used to make employment decisions or to monitor employees without their consent.

Lack of transparency: Many AI systems are opaque and difficult to understand, which can make it difficult for employees to understand how decisions are being made and to challenge unfair or biased outcomes. This lack of transparency can also make it difficult for regulators to hold companies accountable for unethical or illegal practices.

Power imbalances: The use of AI in the workplace can create power imbalances between employers and employees. AI systems can give employers greater control and monitoring capabilities, which could result in exploitation and abuse if not properly managed.

Ethical decision-making: As AI systems become more sophisticated, they may be asked to make ethical decisions on behalf of humans. This raises questions about who is responsible for these decisions and how they should be made.

Security risks: As AI systems become more integrated into workplace systems and processes, they may also become a target for hackers and cybercriminals. This could result in significant security risks for both employees and employers.

Lack of accountability: AI systems can sometimes produce unexpected or unintended outcomes, which can be difficult to predict or prevent. This can make it challenging to hold companies accountable for the actions of their AI systems, particularly if the outcomes are harmful or unethical.\

Unintended consequences: The use of AI in the workplace can have unintended consequences that may not be immediately apparent. For example, the use of AI to optimize productivity may lead to increased stress and burnout among workers, which can have negative impacts on their health and well-being.

Cultural and social impacts: The use of AI in the workplace can have significant cultural and social impacts, particularly if it leads to the erosion of traditional employment models or the displacement of workers from certain industries. This could have ripple effects throughout society, including on income inequality and social mobility.

Lack of human touch: AI systems can automate many aspects of work, but they cannot replace the human touch. This can lead to a loss of human connection and empathy in the workplace, which can have negative impacts on morale and job satisfaction.

Technological dependency: The growing reliance on AI in the workplace can create a sense of technological dependency, where workers become overly reliant on AI systems and lose their ability to think critically or make decisions independently.

This can have negative impacts on creativity, innovation, and problem-solving skills.

CHAPTER THIRTEEN

AI and Creativity

AI has the potential to enhance creativity in various ways. With its ability to analyze and process large amounts of data, AI can assist humans in generating new ideas, improving existing ones, and even creating entirely new works of art.

One way AI can enhance creativity is through generative AI models. These models use deep learning algorithms to generate new content, such as music, images, and text. For example, some generative models can create new music by analyzing existing songs and composing new ones based on the patterns and structures they find. Similarly, some generative models can generate new images or artwork by learning the styles and themes of existing works and creating new ones based on that knowledge.

AI can also enhance creativity by providing new tools for artists and designers. For example, some AI tools can assist in the design process by suggesting new color palettes, layouts, and other design elements based on an artist's preferences. Similarly, some AI-powered writing tools can suggest new word choices, sentence structures.

An Exploration of the role of AI in Creativity

AI is increasingly being used to enhance creativity and generate new forms of art, music, and literature. Through the use of machine learning and deep learning algorithms, AI is able to analyze and learn from large datasets, allowing it to generate new content that is often surprising and original.

One area where AI has shown significant promise is in the creation of visual art. Generative adversarial networks (GANs) are a type of AI algorithm that can generate new images by learning the patterns and features of existing images. These algorithms work by pitting two neural networks against each other: one network generates new images, while the other network tries to determine whether the images are real or fake. Over time, the generator network becomes more skilled at creating images that can fool the discriminator network, resulting in images that are increasingly realistic and original.

AI is also being used to create music. Deep learning algorithms can be trained on large datasets of existing music, allowing them to learn the patterns and structures that are common to different genres of music. Once trained, these algorithms can generate new pieces of music that are similar in style to the music in the original dataset. Some musicians are also using AI to assist in the composition process, using AI tools to generate new melodies or harmonies that they can then incorporate into their own music.

In literature, AI is being used to generate new works of fiction and poetry. Some AI algorithms are capable of analyzing existing works of literature to learn the patterns and structures that are common to different genres and authors. Once trained, these algorithms can generate new works of fiction or poetry that are similar in style to the original works. Some authors are also using AI to assist in the writing process, using AI-powered writing tools to suggest new word choices or sentence structures.

While AI is certainly capable of generating new forms of art, music, and literature, some critics have raised concerns about the role of AI in creative expression. Some argue that AI-generated content lacks the emotional depth and nuance of human-created works, and that it could ultimately lead to a devaluation of human creativity. Others point out that AI-generated content is often created by machines that are trained on large datasets of existing works, which could limit the diversity of new content that is generated.

Despite these concerns, the role of AI in creativity is likely to continue to grow in the coming years. As AI algorithms become more sophisticated and capable of generating more complex forms of content, we may see entirely new forms of art, music, and literature emerge that were previously unimaginable.

Discussion of the Potential Benefits and Challenges of using AI in Creative Field

The use of artificial intelligence (AI) in creative fields has the potential to bring significant benefits, but also raises important ethical questions and challenges that must be addressed. While AI-generated content can be highly impressive and innovative, it can also lack the emotional depth and complexity of human creativity. Additionally, AI-generated content can be influenced by existing biases or stereotypes, or create new ones. In this longer discussion, we will explore these issues in more depth.

One potential benefit of using AI in creative fields is the increased productivity it can bring. For example, AI can assist writers and artists in generating new ideas or compositions more quickly than they might be able to do alone. This can be especially helpful for content creators who are working under tight deadlines or have other constraints on their time. Additionally, AI can help to automate certain aspects of the creative process, such as color selection or layout design, freeing up more time for human creators to focus on more complex or nuanced aspects of their work.

Another potential benefit of using AI in creative fields is the potential to enhance creativity. While AI-generated content may not be as emotionally rich or nuanced as human-generated content, it can still inspire new ideas and perspectives. By using AI to generate unexpected or unconventional ideas, human creators may be able to push the boundaries of what is possible in their respective fields, generating new and exciting content that would not have been possible without the assistance of AI.

However, there are also important challenges associated with the use of AI in creative fields. One of the most significant challenges is the potential impact on human creativity. Some critics argue that the use of AI in creative fields could lead to a devaluation of human creativity, as machines are able to generate content that is often surprising and original, but may lack the emotional depth and nuance of human-created works. This could lead to a reduction in the value placed on human creativity, which could have a negative impact on society as a whole.

Another important challenge associated with the use of AI in creative fields is the potential for bias. AI-generated content is often created using machine learning algorithms that are trained on large datasets of existing works. If these datasets are biased in any way, the resulting AI-generated content may also be biased, perpetuating harmful stereotypes or reinforcing existing inequalities. For example, if an AI algorithm is trained on a dataset of artwork that is predominantly created by white male artists, the resulting AI-generated content may also favor the styles and themes of white male artists, neglecting the contributions of artists from other backgrounds.

Additionally, there are concerns around the ownership and intellectual property of AI-generated content. As AI algorithms become more capable of generating original content, there are questions about who owns the rights to that content. Should the AI algorithm itself be considered the creator, or should the human who trained the algorithm be considered the creator? This is a complex and nuanced issue that has yet to be fully resolved.

Exploration of how to use AI to Enhance creativity and create new forms of art and media

The use of AI in creative fields can lead to exciting new possibilities for the creation of art and media. By utilizing machine learning algorithms and other AI techniques, creators can enhance their own creativity and develop new and innovative forms of expression. Here are some ways in which AI can be used to enhance creativity and create new forms of art and media:

Generative art: AI can be used to create generative art, which involves algorithms that generate art based on a set of predefined rules. Generative art can produce highly complex and dynamic artworks that would be difficult or impossible to create by hand. Artists can use machine learning algorithms to create generative art that evolves over time, or they can use AI to create unique compositions based on user input or other variables.

Music creation: AI can also be used to create music, either by assisting human composers in generating new compositions or by generating music autonomously. For example, AI can be used to analyze large datasets of music to identify patterns and generate new melodies or chord progressions. This can be especially helpful for composers who are looking to experiment with new styles or genres.

Visual effects and animation: AI can also be used to create sophisticated visual effects and animations for film, TV, and other media. Machine learning algorithms can be used to generate realistic simulations of natural phenomena, such as water, fire, or weather, which can be incorporated into films or other media. AI can also be used to create highly detailed and lifelike 3D models and characters, which can be animated using AI-powered tools.

Personalization: AI can be used to create highly personalized content for individual users. For example, AI algorithms can analyze a user's browsing history or social media activity to identify their preferences and interests, and then generate personalized content based on those preferences. This can include personalized music playlists, tailored news articles, or even custom art or graphics.

Augmented reality: AI can be used to create augmented reality experiences that overlay digital content onto the real world. For example, AI algorithms can be used to identify objects in the real world and then generate digital content that interacts with those objects. This can include games, interactive installations, or other forms of media.

Collaborative creation: AI can be used to facilitate collaborative creation, allowing artists and creators from around the world to work together on projects in real-time. For example, AI algorithms can be used to analyze a user's input and generate suggestions for how to improve their work or collaborate with others. This can help artists and creators to discover new perspectives and ideas, and to collaborate with people they might not have had the opportunity to work with otherwise.

Interactive storytelling: AI can be used to create interactive stories that adapt to the user's input and preferences. For example, AI algorithms can be used to analyze a user's choices and generate new storylines or characters based on those choices. This can create a highly immersive and personalized storytelling experience that is tailored to the user's individual interests and preferences.

Image and video analysis: AI can be used to analyze and interpret images and videos in new and innovative ways. For example, AI algorithms can be used to identify patterns or themes in large datasets of images or videos, which can be used to inform creative projects. This can include analyzing the color palettes or composition of images, or identifying common themes or motifs across a series of images or videos.

Creative assistance: AI can be used to assist artists and creators in their work, providing suggestions or feedback to help improve their work. For example, AI algorithms can be used to analyze an artist's style or technique, and then generate suggestions for how to improve or refine their work. This can be especially helpful for artists who are just starting out, or who are looking to explore new techniques or styles.

Data visualization: AI can be used to create sophisticated data visualizations that can help to communicate complex information in a more accessible and engaging way. For example, AI algorithms can be used to analyze large datasets and then generate visualizations that highlight key insights or patterns in the data. This can be used to create compelling infographics or other forms of data-driven media.

While the use of AI in creative fields can lead to exciting new possibilities, it is also important to be mindful of the potential challenges and ethical considerations associated with the use of AI. For example, there is a risk that AI-generated content could be biased or perpetuate stereotypes if the data used to train the algorithms is biased. Additionally, there is a concern that the use of AI could lead to the automation of creative work, potentially displacing human creators from their jobs.

To address these concerns, it is important to work towards solutions that are both innovative and responsible. This may include developing new tools and techniques for addressing bias in AI-generated content, or creating new models for collaboration and shared ownership in creative projects. Overall, the use of AI in creative fields has the potential to transform the way we create and experience art and media, and it will be important to approach these opportunities with a thoughtful and ethical approach.

CHAPTER FOURTEEN

AI and Personal Development

Artificial intelligence (AI) has the potential to revolutionize personal development by providing new tools and resources that can help individuals learn, grow, and achieve their goals. Here are some ways in which AI can support personal development:

Personalized learning: AI can be used to personalize the learning experience, providing tailored feedback and guidance based on an individual's unique learning needs and preferences. For example, AI algorithms can analyze a learner's performance on assessments and provide feedback on areas where they need to improve.

Self-reflection: AI can be used to facilitate self-reflection and self-awareness by analyzing data about an individual's behavior, attitudes, and emotions. For example, AI algorithms can analyze an individual's social media activity and provide insights into their personality and values.

Mental health support: AI can be used to provide mental health support by analyzing data about an individual's behavior and providing insights and recommendations for improving their mental health. For example, AI algorithms can analyze an individual's sleep patterns, exercise habits, and social media activity and provide recommendations for improving their overall well-being.

Goal setting and tracking: AI can be used to help individuals set and track their goals. For example, AI algorithms can analyze an individual's performance data and provide feedback on progress towards their goals. This can help individuals stay motivated and on track towards achieving their goals.

Time management: AI can be used to help individuals manage their time more effectively by analyzing their behavior and providing recommendations for how to optimize their schedule. For example, AI algorithms can analyze an individual's calendar and suggest changes to their schedule to maximize their productivity.

Language learning: AI can be used to support language learning by providing individualized feedback on pronunciation and grammar, as well as personalized language exercises and content. For example, AI-powered language learning platforms can provide real-time feedback on a learner's pronunciation and suggest improvements based on their individual speech patterns.

Decision-making: AI can be used to support decision-making by providing insights and recommendations based on data analysis. For example, AI-powered decision-making tools can analyze data about an individual's past decisions and provide recommendations for future decisions based on patterns and trends.

Personalized coaching: AI can be used to provide personalized coaching in a variety of fields, including sports, music, and public speaking. For example, AI-powered coaching platforms can analyze a learner's performance data and provide tailored feedback and guidance to help them improve their skills.

Emotional intelligence: AI can be used to support emotional intelligence by analyzing data about an individual's behavior and providing insights and recommendations for improving their emotional well-being. For example, AI-powered emotional intelligence tools can analyze an individual's communication patterns and provide feedback on areas where they could improve their emotional intelligence.

Creativity: AI can be used to enhance creativity by providing tools and resources for generating new ideas and content. For example, AI-powered creativity tools can analyze patterns and trends in existing art, music, and literature, and generate new works based on these patterns.

While the potential benefits of using AI for personal development are significant, there are also potential risks and ethical considerations that need to be taken into account. For example, the use of AI for decision-making could result in unintended consequences if the data used to train the algorithms is biased or incomplete. Additionally, there is a risk that AI-generated insights and recommendations could be misinterpreted or lead to unintended consequences if they are not communicated effectively.

To address these concerns, it is important to approach the use of AI in personal development with a thoughtful and ethical approach. This may include developing new tools and techniques for addressing bias in AI-generated insights, or creating new models for data ownership and privacy. Additionally, it will be important to invest in ongoing research and development to ensure that AI technologies continue to be used in ways that support personal development and contribute to the greater good.

An Overview of how AI is being used to Support Personal Development

AI has the potential to transform personal development by providing personalized support and guidance that is tailored to the needs and goals of individuals. With the help of AI, individuals can receive feedback, insights, and recommendations that are based on data analysis, helping them to make more informed decisions and achieve their goals more effectively.

One of the key benefits of using AI in personal development is its ability to provide personalized support and guidance. AI chatbots and coaching apps can be customized to meet the specific needs and goals of individuals, providing them with personalized feedback and advice. For example, an AI-powered chatbot for managing stress may offer relaxation exercises and meditation techniques that are tailored to an individual's specific needs, while a coaching app for fitness may offer personalized workout plans based on an individual's fitness level, goals, and preferences.

Another benefit of using AI in personal development is its ability to analyze large amounts of data quickly and accurately. By analyzing data from sources such as wearables, social media, and online surveys, AI can provide insights and recommendations that would be difficult or time-consuming for a human coach or mentor to generate. For example, an AI-powered financial planning app may analyze an individual's spending patterns and provide personalized recommendations for budgeting and saving, based on their specific financial goals and situation.

AI can also be used to support language learning by providing personalized language exercises and content. AI-powered language learning apps use algorithms to analyze a learner's language skills and provide tailored feedback and guidance. These apps also use AI to personalize language exercises and content, such as articles and videos, to ensure that learners are exposed to content that is relevant to their level and interests.

In addition to providing personalized support and guidance, AI can also be used to support decision-making by providing insights and recommendations based on data analysis. AI-powered decision-making tools can be used in fields such as career development and education to provide guidance on important decisions, such as choosing a career path or selecting a course of study.

However, the use of AI in personal development also poses challenges and risks that need to be addressed. One of the biggest challenges is the potential for bias in AI-generated insights and recommendations. If the data used to train the algorithms is biased or incomplete, it can lead to recommendations that reinforce existing biases or perpetuate inequality. Additionally, there is a risk that AI-generated insights and recommendations could be misinterpreted or lead to unintended consequences if they are not communicated effectively.

To address these challenges, it is important to approach the use of AI in personal development with a responsible and ethical mindset. This may involve developing new tools and techniques for addressing bias in AI-generated insights, or creating new models for data ownership and privacy. It is also important to ensure that individuals have control over their data and are aware of how it is being used.

How AI is being used to Improve Mental Health, Develop New Skills and Promote Personal Growth

AI has the potential to revolutionize personal development, offering new ways to improve mental health, develop new skills, and promote personal growth. Here are some additional examples of how AI is being used in these areas:

Cognitive Behavioral Therapy (CBT) Apps: CBT is a type of talk therapy that has been shown to be effective in treating mental health issues such as depression and anxiety. AI-powered CBT apps use machine learning algorithms to personalize therapy sessions and provide feedback to users.

For example, the app Wysa uses AI to provide users with cognitive behavioral therapy techniques, mindfulness exercises, and other mental health tools.

Personalized Nutrition Apps: AI-powered nutrition apps use machine learning algorithms to analyze users' dietary habits and provide personalized recommendations for improving their diet. These apps can be used to promote physical health and personal growth. For example, Nutrino uses AI to create personalized meal plans based on users' health goals, dietary preferences, and food restrictions.

Language Learning Apps: AI-powered language learning apps use machine learning algorithms to personalize language learning content and exercises based on users' strengths and weaknesses. These apps can be used to develop new skills and promote personal growth. For example, Babbel uses AI to personalize language learning content based on users' previous learning experiences and progress.

Mental Health Diagnostics: AI-powered mental health diagnostics use machine learning algorithms to analyze patterns in data from electronic health records and other sources to predict which individuals are at risk of mental health issues. This technology can be used to identify individuals who may benefit from early intervention or treatment. For example, the company Ginger.io uses AI to predict which individuals may experience depression and other mental health issues based on patterns in their smartphone usage.

Career Development: AI-powered career development platforms use machine learning algorithms to analyze users' skills, work experience, and career goals to provide personalized recommendations for career development opportunities. These platforms can be used to promote personal growth and professional development. For example,

LinkedIn uses AI to provide personalized job recommendations and career advice based on users' interests and skills.

Personalized Fitness Coaching: AI-powered fitness coaching uses machine learning algorithms to analyze data from wearables and other sources to provide personalized coaching and recommendations for improving fitness. This technology can be used to promote physical health and personal growth. For example, the company Vi uses AI to provide personalized coaching and motivation for runners.

Overall, AI has the potential to offer personalized, scalable, and affordable solutions for personal development. While there are challenges to be addressed, such as the potential for bias and the need for data privacy, AI offers exciting possibilities for improving mental health, developing new skills, and promoting personal growth.

www.ingramcontent.com/pod-product-compliance
Lightning Source LLC
Chambersburg PA
CBHW041634050326
40689CB00024B/4959